"If there is a special place in hell for me I gladly accept my fate. There is no price too high to pay for a few good minutes of TV."

"It was about time the NDP got back to their more loony roots. For a while there they were coming off all semi-sensible."

"The Liberals could have gone with a battle-tested politician, a former athlete, a world-famous academic or a food-bank founder from the west. They chose the nerd. That's pretty Canadian."

"The Green Party's Elizabeth May is a welcome addition. As any chef will tell you, a little bit of vinegar brightens up the vegetables."

PRAISE FOR RICK MERCER

"No one on TV has done more to teach Canadians about their own country than Mercer." —*Toronto Star*

"Canada's hottest TV comic." —*Maclean's*

"Week after week, Mercer continues to delight with his alternately giddy and cutting political humour." —*Canadian Press*

"Canada's leading political satirist." —*The New York Times*

"It is 2:30 a.m. and I am sitting up in bed reading Rick Mercer . . . I chortle, I chuckle and I laugh so loudly, I'm sure I've annoyed the couple in the next apartment." —Lyn Cockburn, *Edmonton Sun*

RMR
THE PAPERBACK BOOK

RICK MERCER REPORT

THE PAPERBACK BOOK

RICK MERCER

ANCHOR CANADA

Library and Archives Canada Cataloguing in Publication

Mercer, Rick, 1969–
Rick Mercer Report : the book.

ISBN 978-0-385-66518-6
Paperback ISBN: 978-0-385-66519-3

1. Rick Mercer Report (Television program) 2. Canada—Politics and government—1993–2006—Humor. 3. Canada—Politics and government—2006–Humor. 4. Canadian wit and humor (English) I. Title.

FC173.M473 2007 971.07'20207 C2007-903897-2

Photo credits: page 34 (© CP/Fred Chartrand); page 60 (© *National Post* / Kier Gilmour); page 72 (© *National Post*/Peter J. Thompson); page 144 (© iStockphoto); page 161 (© *The Telegram*); page 236 (© CP/Tom Hanson); page 251 (© Minister of Public Works and Government Services/Corporal David McCord). All RMR pictures © Rick Mercer.

Every effort has been made to attribute correctly material reproduced in this book. If errors have unwittingly occurred, the publisher will be happy to correct them in future editions.

Jacket image: John Hryniuk
Cover and book design: Terri Nimmo
Printed and bound in Canada

Published in Canada by
Anchor Canada, a division of
Random House of Canada Limited

Visit Random House of Canada Limited's website:
www.randomhouse.ca

TRANS 10 9 8 7 6 5 4 3 2 1

For the 308 members of Parliament—the good,
the bad, and the indifferent, and in that order.

ACKNOWLEDGEMENTS

This book took a lot of work and I would be lying if I said it was all on my part. I hit the print button and the excellent people at Doubleday Canada did the rest. Every word I had written over the past four years came out of the hard drive and my editor, Tim Rostron, valiantly sorted and cajoled them into an actual-to-goodness book. I couldn't have asked for a better editor if I'd called central casting and told them to send over a funny but brilliant bookish fellow with a penchant for words and a British accent. I thank Tim for making this such an enjoyable experience. The Doubleday team—designer Terri Nimmo, publicist Cathy Paine, and everyone involved in this project—exceeded my high expectations and I thank them for making it happen.

Rick Mercer Report: The Show is not a one-man show, it just looks that way on television.

The writers' room is small and dangerous. Paul Mather, Greg Eckler, Chris Finn, and Tim Steeves do the heavy lifting and make it seem easy week in and week out. If there are funnier men in the country, I haven't met them. If the walls in that room could talk, they would blush and then probably file some sort of harassment suit.

The show itself would never get done if it wasn't for the crackerjack production team of Alan MacGillivray and Marilyn Richardson.

Tom Stanley is RMR's associate producer and researcher. He spends a lot of time on the phone telling people my helmet size. If anyone else on the show gets hit by lightning, Tom has to fill in, because it turns out he can do anything. His secret weapon is Nik Sexton, his right-hand man in a two-man department.

The actual rants are a three-man operation. I write them, John Marshall produces them and cameraman Don Spence shoots them. John has produced everyone in the country at some point and Don can make a parking lot look interesting. The three of us have spent far too much time together in alleys and on the road, but I have enjoyed every minute.

The show itself is directed by Henry Sarwer-Foner. That's why it's the best-looking show on TV.

Mike Burroughs and the talented crew in the CBC graphics department have always gone above and beyond for *RMR*, and usually when we need something we need it yesterday. If Mike designed everything, it would make for a sexier world.

RMR is edited by Alan Maclean. Nobody looks over his shoulder, nobody bothers him, and in fact most people are not allowed in his little windowless room. He makes me look better than I deserve to, so whatever he wants is fine by me.

And then there is George. Seventeen years ago George Anthony travelled to Ottawa and went to a small gas station-turned-theatre in Ottawa to see me perform in a one-man show. It was a pretty rough show and basically featured me on stage ranting about, of all things, the Meech Lake Accord. Despite the fact that I know George had no interest in the Meech Lake Accord, he told me then that I belonged on the CBC. I've been there ever since. Depending on how you look at things, George Anthony gets the credit or the blame.

Gerald Lunz runs the operation at *RMR,* not only as my partner in crime, executive producer and show-runner, but more importantly, as the funniest guy in the room. It is his baby. Gerald produced that first play in Ottawa 17 years ago, and I have been taking his notes ever since. It's the perfect storm.

Contents

INTRODUCTION xii

1 HOW DEMOCRACY WORKS 1
2 KILLING A TREE WITH ELIZABETH MAY 14
3 NOT COMING ANY TIME SOON TO A CINEMA NEAR YOU 15
4 HARPER VS. MARTIN 20
5 AND THAT OTHER GUY 30
6 ON THE ROAD WITH JACK LAYTON 33
7 NETTING JASON KENNEY 34
8 IN SEARCH OF THE TRUTH 38
9 SAVVY TEACHERS' PLAN 47
10 MY NEWFOUNDLAND, RIGHT OR WRONGED 50
11 OFF-ROAD WITH DANNY WILLIAMS 58
12 THE IGGY ENIGMA 60
13 THAT OTHER GUY (II) 70
14 FISHING WITH BOB RAE 71
15 THE TRIALS OF LORD BLACK 72
16 WAXING LYRICAL WITH CONRAD BLACK 80
17 WOULD ALL THE PEOPLE WITH A KNIGHTHOOD PLEASE SHUT UP 81
18 NATIONS WITHIN OUR NATION 82
19 DOG OF A BLOG 91
20 BULLIES 94
21 TALKING TOUGH WITH JEAN CHRÉTIEN 104
22 HAVE YOU SEEN THIS MAN? 105
23 TREATING US LIKE IDIOTS 108
24 SCIENCE FRICTION 124
25 FREEZING WITH DAVID SUZUKI 132
26 SPENDING LIKE CRAZY 134
27 THE UNDEKE-ABLE WOMAN 143
28 SCANDALOUS BEHAVIOUR 144
29 VISITING PAUL MARTIN 159
30 LEST WE FORGET 161
31 IN BED WITH STEPHEN HARPER 168
32 SLEEPING OVER 174
33 SO YOU WANT TO BE A SPEECHWRITER? 175
34 ELECTION FEVER 178
35 CHOOSING THE NERD 190
36 DOGGING DION 199
37 THAT OTHER GUY, AGAIN 200
38 THE RISE AND STUMBLE OF STÉPHANE DION 202
39 ON COURSE WITH ANNE MURRAY 211
40 DOING SOMETHING RIGHT FOR A CHANGE 212
41 A FEW MODEST PROPOSALS 222
42 DIVING WITH ALEXANDRE DESPATIE 237
43 THRONE FOR A LOOP 238
44 IN THE ARMY NOW 246
45 ON A ROLL WITH PIERRE BERTON 263
46 OUR NEIGHBOURS TO THE SOUTH 264
47 CANADA'S NEARLY NEW GOVERNMENT 272
48 THE END 297

INTRODUCTION

The truth is I rarely know where I am going to be from one day to the next. My luggage has remained packed for over a decade and I have more long underwear than any city dweller in his right mind should need.

Over the last five years, while on the job, I have almost lost consciousness midair while doing aeronautics with Canada's Snowbirds, I have experienced intentionally induced hypothermia at the hands of a celebrated university professor in Winnipeg, I have made a five-thousand-foot free fall out of an airplane over Trenton, Ontario, and I have done doughnuts in the middle of Halifax harbour while operating a tugboat. I have faced death (or at the very least the possibility of severed thumbs) when lying "nose down, bum up" on a skeleton sled while hurtling down a bobsled track in Calgary. In Rockland, Ontario, I signed a waiver and got behind the wheel and joined a demolition derby.

My job description includes sleepovers at Stephen Harper's house and getting buck naked with Bob Rae.

Despite the latter two, I am still convinced that I have the best gig in Canadian show business. And through it all I have managed to stay true to my one ultimate career goal—no heavy lifting.

The travel is the best part.

If you are lucky enough to spend time in the North, it will change you. It will inform the way you feel about the country in a way that no amount of reading on the subject ever can. When you spend time eating raw caribou north of the tree line with a politician in Nunavut or listening to an Inuit hunter before he heads out alone on the ice to hunt a polar bear—those things tend to stay with you.

The same can be said for spending time on the Prairies, in Northern Ontario, in Newfoundland, in the oil sands of Alberta, or in any of the many Chinatowns or Little Indias that dot the country.

Canada has so many problems—and geography is often the root cause. For the size of the population, we are simply too bloody big.

I can't count the number of times I've been in a situation where five people were busy complaining about what the problem was with another part of the country that they were happy to admit they had never visited.

I've had cabinet ministers lecture me on why people in Newfoundland should never have control of their natural resources and then in the next breath tell me they have it on good authority that the province is very pretty. Not a surprise, really. Stephen Harper coined the phrase "the culture of defeat" about Atlantic Canada before he bothered to go there.

Ottawa is a place that Canadians love to attack without having set foot there, and God knows everyone in Eastern Canada seems to have an idea of what Calgary is all about without ever having met the people whose drive and determination are responsible for our very own emerging superpower.

There is no simple solution, of course. Again, size is to blame. It's easy to have an opinion on how Canada should deal with an issue in Nunavut, but actually going there requires a time commitment and an airplane ticket. Unfortunately, time and money top the list of what most people don't have enough of.

We live in a country where it's cheaper to fly to Paris than it is to fly a few provinces over and see for ourselves what another part of Canada is really about. More Canadians visit Florida than Manitoba. In a country with unity issues, this does not bode well.

I've been very lucky when it comes to exploring Canada. The show lets me experience another part of the country almost every week. And despite the occasional near-death experience and/or outbreak of nudity, every single week I become more enamoured with the place.

This book is for the most part a collection of commentaries that I have written and performed on the show during the last five seasons or posted on my blog at rickmercer.com. It contains, for lack of a better term, my "rants." When you follow politics in Canada either as a living or because it's just in your blood, you are never short of a reason to rant. The problems are legion and the situations are often absurd. The rants often write themselves. I started ranting about Canada a long time ago and I really don't see any end in sight. It's what I do and I have never lost sight of how fortunate I am to get to do it every week.

And sure, on the surface Canada may appear hopelessly dysfunctional, but the more I rant, the more I realize that we are also spectacular in every sense of the word.

Canada, for all its challenges, is worth ranting about.

Rick Mercer

HOW DEMOCRACY WORKS

In a minority government timing is everything. And when a minority government looks like it's teetering on the brink of collapse, whether actually or imagined, orchestrated or not, you can rest assured that once the structural flaws are exposed a chorus of pundits will start to sing: "Canadians just aren't in the mood for an election." Personally, I am always in the mood for an election—but that's a character flaw of mine. Most hockey fans would be happy with back-to-back playoffs, and that is pretty much the way I feel about elections.

Bring 'em on. It takes ten minutes to vote, folks, and the results are always worth it.

AN UNELECTED IDIOT? | FEB. 2, 2004

I've always thought that the worst thing that could ever happen to Canada would be that somehow a complete idiot got elected as prime minister. And so far we've been pretty lucky. Brian Mulroney was called lots of things, but stupid wasn't usually one of them. And Jean Chrétien made no sense whatsoever, but it turns out he was actually fairly bright.

Which brings us to Prime Minister Paul Martin (not that he was actually elected). Watching him on the job for the last couple of weeks, I think we've all been thinking the same thing: we've seen brighter lights on small appliances.

Here he is, a Liberal prime minister facing a united Conservative right-wing party, perhaps the most serious threat the Liberals have faced in over a decade. And what's he doing? Every time he turns around he's attacking Jack Layton and the NDP. And the more he attacks the NDP, the stronger the NDP gets.

Then it dawned on me: perhaps Martin's no fool. Perhaps he's been boning up on *The Art of War* and he's going to use the NDP to destroy the Conservatives. Sure, Martin would love to stand up and say, "Hey Canada, you want Conservative, vote for me. I'm more Conservative than Brian Mulroney ever was." But he can't say that because the sign on the door to the prime minister's office says Liberal. So how's he going to get that message out? The NDP. So he's doing them every favour he can think of. Hell, he even tried to give them Sheila Copps, and that's a gift that keeps on giving.

So don't worry, Canada—no matter what you think about Paul Martin, at least we know one thing about him: like every great prime minister before him, at least he's not as stunned as he looks.

MINORITY SHOW | OCT. 25, 2004

Over one hundred of the MPs in Canada's 38th Parliament are brand spankin' new. Think about that. A third of our MPs have never done anything like this before in their lives. It's mind-boggling when you consider the layers of dumb that have yet to be revealed to us. Because that's the way it works: if you've got one hundred MPs, I can guarantee you twenty-five of them will be completely off their heads. And this is not me talking here—this is an established law of averages.

Sure, they may look like normal, rational human beings. They might even sound like normal, rational human beings. But that is only because they haven't really said anything yet. But they're in there now, just waiting for the right moment to stand up, open their mouths, humiliate their party and reveal to the world just how completely bonkers they are.

They can belong to any party. That's the beauty of it. And because it's a minority government, they will not be ignored. Their votes are far too important. So important that these unknown loose cannons who walk among us could very well end up running the place. When you think about it, this Parliament is very modern. It's not like a Parliament at all—it's like a reality show. All we've got to figure out now is where Canada fits in the grand scheme of things. In this show, are we the winners, the losers—or the prize?

FOCUS ON DARREL | OCT. 10, 2006

For those of us who enjoy Question Period for its pure theatrical value, it's nice to see that the Liberals are finally hitting their stride. For a while there in opposition they were pathetic. They were about as fierce as a bag of kittens. They finally figured out that their job is to oppose—to attack—but lately they've gone a little bit too far.

This week they were all upset because Rona Ambrose, the minister of the environment, went out and hired this guy Darrel Reid to be her new chief of staff. Now the interesting thing here is, the Liberals aren't upset because the guy's not qualified—they're upset because he's too conservative.

This is where the Liberals lose me. You can't not hire someone because of their views. This is Canada. We have laws against that type of thing. We just elected a Conservative government here, and when the big jobs become available they're going to go to Conservatives. That's just the way it works.

Some people might say, "Hey, the minister of the environment needs a chief of staff—this person is going to run an entire government ministry—we need someone in here who's worked with big business and big environment groups." Not this crowd. The Tories say, "This is a perfect opportunity to give a job to the former president of Focus on the Family."

You remember Focus on the Family. They're the ones who think that SpongeBob SquarePants is gay. Take a look at their website—these people think about gay sex more than gay people do. I only hope that when Darrel Reid is in his new job, he can take his mind off gay sex long enough to think about the plight of the chubsucker, which by the way is an endangered fish and not a lifestyle choice. Of course, that's not all Focus on the Family worries about. They do other good works. Focus on the Family International was one of the first groups to come out and support Mel Gibson after he revealed his views on our Hebrew friends to the world.

Bottom line, though, is that Darrel is a good foot soldier for the Conservative party, and Stephen Harper wants him in Ottawa. In fact, they ran Darrel Reid in the last election. That ended badly when he lost the election and his campaign manager went ballistic and blamed the defeat on the Jews who control the Canadian media. But that's all in the past now. Thanks to Rona Ambrose, Darrel Reid—your Focus on the Family candidate—is going to make it to Ottawa after all.

No surprises there, because this is a democracy, folks—and in Canada you get what you vote for.

APRÈS DION | DEC. 5, 2006

There's no doubt about it: big leadership conventions like the one we just saw in Montreal make for great TV. At least, for someone like me they do.

If you like politics—and I'm certainly guilty of that—you must take your excitement where you can get it. And, tragically, watching a few thousand socially retarded adults jump up and down and wave signs with someone else's name on it is what passes for exciting.

Although, as this convention unfolded, I couldn't help but think that I was not so much watching a vital political party in the midst of renewal as watching a bunch of dinosaurs in their death throes. If this party is not careful, you're looking at a future tar sands site.

The Liberals had a chance at this convention to change the way they choose leaders so that in the future every single member would get a vote. And they took a pass. Now why they would do this I have no idea. Look at

Alberta. The provincial Conservative party there just chose a leader, and 97,000 party members voted on the first ballot. That's just one province. At the Liberal convention in Montreal only 5,000 members voted, and that's for the entire country.

In Alberta it costs five bucks to vote for the leader. Basically they'll take anyone with a pulse. In Montreal it costs almost a thousand bucks to get through the front door, and that does not include airfare, accommodations or escort fees. It adds up. And the only reason the Liberals can come up with as to why they chose to not go with a more open and democratic system is that Canadians like to watch an old-fashioned convention.

Well that may be true, but the problem is that when the Liberals run a convention, that's all Canadians get to do: watch from the sidelines. And politics, when it works, shouldn't be a spectator sport.

RUN, FORTIER, RUN | OCT. 31, 2006

After the last election Stephen Harper got a lot of grief for taking a guy who had never been elected and putting him into cabinet. And sure that looks bad, but it makes sense that in extraordinary circumstances a prime minister should be allowed to appoint non-elected people to cabinet. Imagine if Canada was at war and nobody in the House of Commons happened to have any experience with the army. It makes sense that the prime minister should be able to go out and find experts on the military and put them in cabinet.

Or imagine for a second you're Stephen Harper. You form a government only to find out that most of your MPs aren't smart enough to be cabinet ministers. So of course you've got to have the right to be able to call up your buddy from Montreal and give him the big job. Which is exactly what Stephen Harper did. He called up Michael Fortier, private citizen, and made him a cabinet minister.

You know, that's a very good gig. The man has never been elected to anything, and all of a sudden the rest of us are supposed to refer to him as "the Honourable Michael Fortier" for the rest of his natural life. And when, God forbid, he passes away, the flag on the Peace Tower will be lowered to half mast to honour Michael Fortier's contribution to democracy. It's very touching.

I'm not saying this was easy for Stephen Harper. It must be hard to look all your MPs in the eye and tell them they're imbeciles. And imagine that you were elected to the House of Commons, your party formed the government, and then your leader let you know you had a better chance of picking up a disability cheque based on your own mental incompetence than you ever did of seeing a minister's salary. That's what you call a tough day at the office.

But that was the situation we were in, Canada. Stephen Harper wanted a smart person from Montreal in his cabinet, he didn't have one, so he had to appoint one.

But that was then, and as of right now there is a seat wide open in Montreal. Except Michael Fortier says he doesn't want it. Well, I'm sorry, Michael, the prime minister has called a by-election and the people of Montreal are going to the polls. This is a democracy, baby; this is what it's all about. If you want to keep your seat in the Canadian cabinet, it's time you got a seat in the Canadian House of Commons.

It's one thing for the prime minister to ignore his MPs, that's his right. But no prime minister has the right to ignore the will of the people.

The people of Montreal are going to the polls. The definition of democracy is "one woman, one man, one vote." It's time for Michael Fortier to be man enough to ask the people of Montreal for theirs.

WHO POLLS THE POLLSTERS? | FEB. 26, 2008

Newspapers and newscasts love polls. Every single day we wake up, there's a brand-new set of numbers telling us what the average Canadian thinks, how the average Canadian is going to vote. I find it very entertaining. One minute Harper's numbers are down, the next minute they're up. Same with Dion—one minute they're down, the next minute, well, they're usually down, but you get my point.

But they're not just entertaining. Believe it or not, polls actually matter. Governments decide when they're going to have elections based on the polls. Public policy is dictated by polls, and sometimes Canadians decide how they're going to vote based on the polls. The problem is, it's very easy for the average Canadian to avoid being polled; because, while polling has not changed since the 1960s, the average Canadian certainly has.

For starters, these polling companies, they only call land lines. They don't call cellphones. So right off the bat, if you're under the age of thirty, you don't get called. Your opinion doesn't count. And then of course a lot of Canadians, I'd go so far as to say the average Canadian, just doesn't like to pick up the phone if they don't know who's on the other line. That's why God created call display. And keep in mind, most of these calls are made in the evening between five and nine p.m. So if you have a social life or small kids, or you do shift work, or you happen to like *Jeopardy*, your opinion doesn't count.

Now personally, I would love to be polled. I've been waiting for that phone call for fifteen years—the phone has never rung. Granted, I would spend the entire time lying and saying things like "I believe the Green party is best suited to manage the economy," but at least I'd take the call. Everyone else I know, they'd just hang up.

So who are these people? Who's taking the calls? Who are these people that are affecting public policy? I have no idea, but I know this: when it comes to polling, the average Canadian is far from normal and well below average, give or take 3 per cent, 19 times out of 20.

APATHY SWEEPS THE BY-ELECTIONS | MAR. 25, 2008

This past week was a big one for Canadian democracy. Four federal by-elections in one day. Big stuff when you consider we're a country with a minority government. And the numbers, they tell quite the story. In fact, they tell multiple stories.

For the Conservatives, who picked up one seat, the numbers spelled victory. For the Liberals, who picked up three seats, the numbers spelled victory. And for the NDP, who picked up zero seats, somehow the numbers spelled victory. Apparently, the numbers told more stories than Stephen Harper has personalities.

But one number you didn't hear any of the national leaders talk about was seventy-two. Seventy-two as in 72 per cent. As in 72 per cent of eligible voters didn't vote. They stayed at home. A 72 per cent no-show is not just a case of voter apathy, it's a full-on allergic reaction. The numbers don't lie, and the numbers are telling us the average Canadian voter feels like some guy who can't eat eggs without throwing up being told that his choices are scrambled, fried or poached.

So why aren't any of our national leaders talking about this problem? Well, because it's their fault. They're the ones in the kitchen, and 72 per cent of the electorate, they just don't like what's on the menu. In fact, the only party that has any bragging rights at all after these by-elections is Elizabeth May's Green Party. It's the only party whose numbers went up. And what's more impressive is that people who actually voted for the Greens did so knowing full well that none of their candidates would actually win. Yet they still managed to get out of bed before five or six o'clock in the evening and vote—and for a lot of Green Party members, that's quite the accomplishment.

I'm not saying the Greens are a full-on movement. But at least they're moving, which is more than can be said for the rest of them. And as far as I can tell, it looks like the Greens are here to stay—which is a good thing because Stephen Harper, Stéphane Dion and Jack Layton are looking pretty stale and Elizabeth May is a welcome addition. As any chef will tell you, a little bit of vinegar brightens up the vegetables.

KILLING A TREE WITH ELIZABETH MAY

The leader of the Green Party saws down a very dangerous tree that was threatening to fall on someone's cottage.
Gatineau, Quebec.
Broadcast Oct. 17, 2006

MERCER: The tree is coming down.

MAY: I think we should discuss it.

MERCER: Why?

MAY: Well, because you see that tree represents great habitat for woodpeckers and other cavity-nesting birds.

MERCER: You would risk that tree landing on his mother's cottage? With his mother inside? Because of a woodpecker?

MAY: We've got the habitat for mom and kids versus the habitat for the woodpecker, so—

MERCER: Guess who loses? Let's get the chainsaws.

* * *

MERCER: How'd that feel?

MAY: It's a heady sense of power.

MERCER: This is fantastic. The leader of the Green Party cutting down a tree. It's like Stephen Harper performing a gay marriage.

NOT COMING ANY TIME SOON TO A CINEMA NEAR YOU

MARCH 2, 2008

From the Desk of Prime Minister Stephen Harper

My fellow Conservatives,

As you have no doubt heard, we are now fixing the criteria for tax credits for Canadian movies and TV shows. From now on we can simply deny the tax credits granted to TV and film productions if we find them obscene or in any way personally offensive to our way of life. Make no mistake about it—this is a very large stick we now wield against the entertainment industry. If we deny them tax credits after they have made their projects and spent their money, they could face bankruptcy. I see the future, my friends, and it's starring Anne of Green Gables.

As our good friend Charles McVety said recently, this is a victory that can be directly attributed to his organization the Canada Family Action Coalition. It is through their hard work—and lobbying of our Justice Minister, Vic Toews, and our Minister of Public Safety, Stockwell Day, and numerous officials in my office—that we can now ensure that like-minded conservatives have the final say on what kind of TV shows and movies get made in Canada.

This is just the beginning. Other industries are next. If the Ontario auto sector wants help from this government, then it will have to give cabinet the final say on any new automobile designs.

Environment Minister John Baird's assistant Pierre Poilievre will be our front man on that issue. He works hard, is well qualified and has the entire Hot Wheels collection going back to 1978. He also recently got his learner's permit, so I think we are in good hands. He tells me he has some ideas for the new Ford Mustang—something to do with lasers.

The publishing industry will have to wait until we get a majority. Like you, I look forward to the day when a wise man such as Jim Flaherty can decide what is suitable reading material for all Canadians. Take that Margaret Atwood. Time for some mystery novels, I think.

For the time being, though, we are busy with cleaning up show business. But as the saying goes, no good deed goes unpunished. Now on top of running the country we have to watch all these godforsaken Canadian movies. Who knew there were so many? I certainly didn't.

Today we screened a new one called *Trailer Park Boys.* Not only were we not prepared to grant these people a tax credit, we had no choice but to call the police and initiate an instant review of some channel called Showcase. Poor Stockwell had a seizure during the opening credits and began to hyperventilate into a brown paper bag.

My friends, cutting off tax credits and bankrupting a company is not a decision I make lightly; luckily *Trailer Park Boys* seems to have been made by a company in Atlantic Canada, so that's okay. This *Trailer Park* business just reinforces my belief that the region is mired in a culture of defeat. As I said to Chuck Strahl, our Minister of Indian Affairs—instead of glorifying drugs and violence, they should simply make a nice show like *The Forest Rangers.* Chuck agreed, offering the kind of insight that makes him one of my most trusted ministers: "You got that right, boss, that Bubbles is no Indian Joe Two Rivers."

Helena Guergis had a good idea that could save the production. "Why not add a talking car," she said, "like Herbie the Love Bug?" Helena loves Herbie. When she was sworn in as Parliamentary Secretary for Foreign Affairs she proudly informed cabinet that she was up to the job and that *Herbie Goes to Monte Carlo* was her favourite movie of like all time.

We were about to pencil in the talking car note, but as luck would have it John Baird is also a Herbie aficionado and he reported that the Love Bug did not in fact speak in sentences but communicated by honking his horn, blinking his lights and slamming his hood up and down—a communication technique John admires greatly.

Throwing his panic bag aside, a horrified Stockwell Day shouted that we could not in good conscience give a tax credit to any project involving a talking car; that such behaviour in a Volkswagen clearly indicated that Herbie was possessed by Satan. He told us the only thing that would fix that Love Bug was a run through a carwash of holy water. This led Peter MacKay to inform us that when he was in university, a "love bug" meant that it hurt when you peed. Peter goes too far sometimes. He tortures Stockwell any chance he can get. Those two are always at it. If it's not arguing over how best to proceed in the Middle East, it's who looks better in fatigues.

Anyway, we decided that the *Trailer Park* movie could be saved, but only if all the scenes involving drugs, sex, guns and premarital sex were removed. It comes in at two and a half minutes now. The only things left are shots of Bubbles and his kittens. Like Bubbles, I love kittens! I wish more people would make movies that are about kittens or puppies or rabbits. The film character I relate to most is Lenny in *Of Mice and Men*. He loved to stroke soft animals but he didn't know his own strength. I can identify with that, let me tell you. Every time I pick up one of the sixty-four kittens now using 24 Sussex as a litter box, Laureen says, "Watch it, Lenny . . . remember what happened last time."

The next movie we had to watch was introduced by Vic Toews, President of the Treasury Board. He was livid. He reported that it was the latest sequel to the most successful film franchise in Quebec. In hushed and serious tones, he told us that the movie was a lurid and violent tale about lesbian boys. He was very concerned that the agenda of the entertainment industry has moved past simply turning our sons gay and is now concentrating on turning them into lesbians. It was quite a bombshell. Lesbian boys? It boggles the mind what passes for entertainment in Quebec.

Vic wanted an immediate vote on the movie without screening it. As he said, the title was all he needed to know that some tough justice was required to drive this Quebec company out of business *tout de suite!* (Uh oh—Vic's working on his French.) Vic was shouted down by Gary Lunn, who was sitting next to him. Gary jumped up on his chair, stared straight up at Vic and said, "I want to see the lesbians!" I am relieved to report that Vic was a bit confused, and that the movie was in fact called *Les Boys*. It's about hockey players. This will get the tax credit, but we must change the title and remove the swearing and the sex.

Next up was, can you believe it, yet another Trudeau biopic from the CBC, this one titled *Trudeau: The Bi-Curious Years*. I always suspected the man was a bisexual. Rumour has it he had sex with Barbra Streisand in the pool at 24. (Note to self: have Dimitris call Public Works and have the pool drained and repainted.) This got the tax credit and will no doubt be aired by the

CBC seventeen times over the next six months. Oh well, it's their funeral.

The pleasant surprise of the evening was a movie written by our very own Government House Leader, Peter Van Loan, under his pseudonym Debbie Vanderlear. It is a modern retelling of *My Fair Lady* about a handsome young man at university who mentors young women in conservative ideology. The man (a cross between Brad Pitt and Barney Rubble) dreams of finding a girl and grooming her to become the prime minister of Canada. After numerous attempts he gives them all the creeps and so has to become prime minister himself. I told him it would get the tax credit as long as they cut the last part where he becomes prime minister. This isn't science fiction, Peter.

Other highlights of the meeting included killing a David Cronenberg movie, killing a Paul Gross movie and killing a Sarah Polley movie (they have all said bad things about me lately, and the sooner they move on, the better). Also we put the kibosh on some kids' movie about the carbon-dating of dinosaurs (too far-fetched).

Our next meeting of the Conservative film club is in one week. Until then, God bless Canada and save the aisle seat for me.

Yours truly,

Stephen Harper

HARPER VS. MARTIN

It is the unknown that makes politics exciting. It's like baseball that way: there are more pundits than players and occasionally nobody gets it right.

It was not so long ago that Paul Martin seemed destined to become an unbeatable prime minister who would deliver record majorities to the Liberal Party of Canada. His only foe was Stephen Harper, who by all accounts was an unlikable, uncharismatic leader destined to waste a few years in the opposition benches until the Conservatives could find someone electable to replace him. Times changed. Paul Martin left public life to spend quality time with his money, and Canada became governed by the angry dad.

BE STRAIGHT WITH US, STEPHEN | DEC. 6, 2005

The federal election campaign has finally officially begun. After sizing up the week-one performances of both the Tories and the Liberals, all I can say is this: Wow, what a pack of arseholes.

The prime minister of Canada starts off the campaign of his lifetime by acting hurt because the Tories have said the Liberals are in bed with organized crime. Paul, I hate to break it to you, brother, but nobody cares if people call you names. In fact, everyone in Canada has used far worse words to describe the Liberals than anything Stephen Harper is allowed to say on television in prime time.

Stephen Harper, to give him credit, has set the agenda since day one. He came out swinging and made it loud and clear that his number-one priority was that he, Stephen Harper, was against gay marriage. Thanks for the clarification there, Stephen. We get it. Despite the poofy new hairdo, the full makeup and the mock turtlenecks, you're not gay. Let it go.

Eventually, of course, he started talking about something people care about: tax reduction. And why not? A Stephen Harper government would reduce the GST to 5 per cent. And just to drive that point home Stephen Harper walked into a grocery store, covered up the 7 per cent GST sign with his own 5 per cent GST sign. A very sexy photo op, leading one to believe that if he becomes prime minister, he will reduce the GST to 5 per cent. Not true. Read the fine print. Stephen Harper will reduce the GST to 5 per cent *in 2011.* The year two thousand and eleven—when we're all driving hovercars and eating dehydrated turkey pills.

Stephen, why don't you do us a favour? Tell us what you'll do for us if you win this election, not the one that's going to happen five years from now.

So all in all, not a bad start. Basically: name-calling, BS and outright lies. My advice is that both parties should go to their corners, think about what they've done, turn around, come out and start all over again.

NEW MEDS, PLEASE | FEB. 14, 2005

Parliament's been back in session for two whole weeks now and I'm guessing that at any moment Canadians might actually notice. But I've got to tell you—as far as sessions go, this one has been very exciting. Every day, Stephen Harper and Prime Minister Martin are in there hammering at one another on the major issues of the day.

And never before have their positions been so clear. Look at Iraq. The big rumour is that at any moment George Bush is going be on the phone asking Canada to send forty troops to help train Iraqi soldiers. You'd think

Stephen Harper would be all over this. After all, he was the guy who stood up in the House of Commons before the war and wanted Canada to send our army into Baghdad guns a-blazing. When he heard about the coalition of the willing, he was so willing he almost wet his pants.

But now, apparently, he's had a change of heart. He says he's against the operation, and if Bushy calls we've got to say, hell no, we won't go. Harper is like a goldfish. He says one thing on one side of the bowl, and by the time he's turned around and swum to the other side of the bowl he's completely forgotten what he said over there and has to make up something new. To cover himself, he's saying this time that he's against sending forty troops to Iraq, unless, of course, he can become personally convinced that they will be 100 per cent safe and then they can go.

Does this guy even watch the news? It's Iraq—of course it's not going to be safe. Armies don't get sent to safe places. That's the whole point of armies. It's easy, Stephen: find a guy in uniform, ask him. But at least we know where Harper stands on the issue. He's against it, unless he's for it.

And what about Prime Minister Martin? What's his opinion? Who knows. He's got this new trick on the go where any time he's asked a direct question, he acts so completely baffled nobody knows what the hell he's talking about and then he gets really excited or really sad. Yes, watching these two guys go at it is like watching two superheroes. Although it's not so much good versus evil, it's ADD boy versus bipolar man.

The future's clear, Canada. We need new meds.

MARTIN CAN TAKE A PUNCH | FEB. 28, 2005

Prime Minister Martin finally got some good news last week and my guess is, he's more surprised than anyone.

The week started out the way most weeks do for Paul Martin, with lots of bad news. The biggie being *The Economist* magazine, which called him Mr. Dithers. For most of us, *The Economist* is something we might accidentally see on a newsstand, but for Martin, this is brutal. He looks at *The Economist* the way teenage boys look at *Maxim*. Yet the same week, out of the blue, for no reason, his personal approval rating went up.

Now I follow these things, and for the life of me I can't figure out why this happened. Conventional wisdom says that if you're the prime minister and you do something clever or smooth, your numbers go up. Likewise, if you act like Paul Martin, your numbers should go down. But not this time.

The poor old Tories must be ready to jump off a bridge, because compared to Martin, Harper couldn't look more like a leader if he'd been whipped up in a lab. With Martin, you ask him a simple question, he breaks out in bumps, whereas Harper is so calm it's freakish. He's the kind of guy who could have his foot caught in a thresher and he'd just carry on like everything was normal.

All I can figure is that Canadians are starting to admire Martin in the same way that we admire someone who can take a punch. He's like George Chuvalo. He's standing there taking blow after blow to the head. And we know he should be spitting out teeth and hitting the mat, but nope, Martin just stands there with a great big goofy grin on his face.

In many ways this is very Canadian. When push comes to shove, the trait that we most admire in a leader is not honesty, integrity or grace under pressure. It's who can take the biggest smack.

HARPER'S DULL EDGE | MAR. 7, 2005

Conservatives all across the country are gearing up for what could be the very exciting founding convention of the Conservative party.

Yes, I find these things exciting. Bear with me.

This is the official opposition, and yet the actual members of the two parties that merged to form this new party have never been together in a room before. And the exciting part is, they hate each other. Stick 'em in a room, give 'em a few drinks, the place could go up—total implosion.

I know, Conservatives always say the same thing: that too much is being made of the fact that there are differences of opinion in the Conservative party. That we should focus on what they agree on, not what they disagree on. And they love to point out that there are deep divisions inside the rank and file of the Liberal party—which is true but doesn't matter, because the Liberals, when push comes to shove, will always stick together.

Unlike the Conservatives, the Liberals would sell their own mothers to stay in power. In fact, I believe that is the founding principle of the Liberal Party of Canada: "We'll sell our mothers." It's in Latin on a crest somewhere.

The Conservatives are the total opposite. They would rather self-destruct than compromise just a little bit. That's what they've done for over a decade. In many ways, it's what they do best. In fact, that could be their founding principle: "We rise up, and then we screw up."

Maybe this time it will be different. Stephen Harper is the leader now, he's going to give the keynote address and there's no doubt about it—he can suck all the energy out of a room. So maybe this time duller heads will prevail, and at the end of the day they'll come out of this thing more united than ever before. For the sake of the party I hope that's true. But you have to admit, it wouldn't be much fun, would it?

PRETTY UNLUCKY | AUG. 8, 2006

The Tory caucus gathered in Toronto last week for a miniature policy retreat, and something truly shocking happened: policy was announced. This is a big departure for the opposition and it could have severe consequences. If they keep this up, people might confuse them with a national party.

The big news is, the Conservatives are proposing a

$400 million tax break for people who use public transit. It's aimed directly at big-city urban voters. When I heard this, I couldn't really believe it—because, well, it makes so much sense. In fact, it makes so much sense that I can only assume the Liberals will have stolen it by this time next week.

Unfortunately, Harper's announcement didn't cause much of a stir in the media because, in the battle for space on the front page, the Tories once again had their asses kicked. As luck would have it, on the day Harper was making his public transit announcement in Toronto, Paul Martin was in Ottawa introducing Canada's new governor general, Michaëlle Jean.

To be fair, Harper tried his damnedest to compete with the prime minister's photo op. He invited the media to take pictures of him getting off a Toronto streetcar with his son. In Harper's world that is pretty dynamic stuff.

You can't really blame the newspapers on this one. When it comes to photos, Michaëlle Jean is just downright way better looking and more interesting than Stephen Harper, no matter what character from the Village People he happens to be dressed as. It must have been devastating for him, though, when he saw that practically every paper in the country ran with the picture of Michaëlle Jean instead of the one of him on the streetcar. Of course it didn't hurt that our new GG just happens to have the cutest daughter in Canada.

Somewhere Stephen Harper is yelling at his son, "Next time be cuter, damn it!"

AND THAT OTHER GUY

TIME FOR LAYTON TO STEP UP | MAR. 21, 2005

When the Liberals said no to American missile defence, there were more than a few Canadians who were seriously pissed off. But I can't imagine there was anyone more devastated than Jack Layton.

Now, if you don't know who Jack Layton is, that's okay, it's not your fault, you're in the majority. Jack is the leader of the NDP. And really, he only had one thing going for him. He was against missile defence when everyone else seemed to be for it. Then in one fell swoop, the Liberals put the kibosh on missile defence and took Jack out right at the knees. In fact, I would say missile defence was Jack's entire *raison d'être,* which is French for "He's now screwed."

And the NDP, they're not just screwed, it's worse than that. They're invisible. In fact, the only press Jack got in the last three months was when his appendix burst. In politics, it is a very bad sign if you're the leader of a national party and the only way you can get your name in the paper is to go in for emergency surgery and get your parts shaved. Next thing you know you're standing up in the House of Commons and all anyone is thinking is, boy, he must be itchy.

I'm assuming of course that Jack does stand up in the House of Commons. You'd never know from watching the news. Who knows, maybe there's a media conspiracy designed to keep Jack down. Somehow I doubt it, though. I think it's a case of dull is dull and dull does not lead. The man hasn't even been thrown out of the House of Commons for calling the prime minister a liar yet. That was standard operating procedure for the NDP. If I was leader of the NDP I'd do that three times a week. That's what Canadians want. A strong, lippy NDP. Even people on the right want a strong NDP.

But by strong, Jack, we mean from the left, not the centre. Shag the centre. The centre's full and so is the right. Canadians want one thing and one thing only from the NDP: a pit bull for a leader who is not afraid to go out there and make an arse out of himself in the name of social justice. The job's yours, Jack, time to start doing it.

THE LAYTON-TALIBAN TALKS | SEPT. 6, 2006

I see that Jack Layton has distinguished himself on the international front by coming up with a solution for the Afghanistan situation. Jack is calling for peace talks with the Taliban. It was about time the NDP got back to their more loony roots. For a while there they were coming off all semi-sensible.

Rest assured. If there are peace talks between the Taliban and Jack Layton, *Rick Mercer Report* will be there. I've attended a lot of political events over the years, and as a location for the Layton-Taliban talks I would suggest one of the ballrooms at the casino in

Hull. I think you might be able to smoke there, and I'm guessing the Taliban would appreciate that. All the Taliban really needs for a good time is an ashtray and a few de-peopled women making sure there's a steady supply of unsafe drinking water.

Agenda for historic peace talks between Jack Layton and Taliban leader—Room 202, Casino Du Lac Leamy, Quebec

8:00 a.m.—Jack Layton: opening comments and welcome to assembled media and Taliban representative.

8:05 a.m.—Taliban representative walks to podium, poses for photographs with Mr. Layton.

8:06 a.m.—Taliban representative cleaves Mr. Layton in the forehead with giant axe.

8:08 a.m.—Peace talks end.

8:10 a.m.—Olivia Chow says she is "encouraged by talks"—announces plan to run for leadership of NDP.

ON THE ROAD WITH JACK LAYTON

On an NDP tour.
Broadcast Jan. 23, 2006

MERCER: I heard you brought the guitar out a few times.

LAYTON: We did. A few times.

MERCER: Jack, Jack, you can't go doing that, Jack.

LAYTON: Why not?

MERCER: What songs did you do?

LAYTON: We went back to the sixties . . .

MERCER: Oh.

LAYTON: . . . we sang the old Bob Dylan stuff . . .

MERCER: Oh, Jack.

LAYTON: . . . *The Times They Are A-Changin'* was a big hit.

MERCER: Oh Jack, you're killing me. What else?

LAYTON: Well, we did get on to *Barrett's Privateers*.

MERCER: Did you pass out song sheets?

LAYTON: Song *books.*

MERCER: Oh! Jack! *Mother!*

LAYTON: How about if we gave you the tambourine?

MERCER: Oh great. Or a jar with lentils in, that's a good NDP instrument.

NETTING JASON KENNEY

JUNE 24, 2005

Is there a God? In the midst of a slow news week in the summer of 2005, Jason Kenney, Member of Parliament for Calgary Southeast, gave me all the evidence I would ever need.

Listening to Jason pontificate in the Commons with all the wisdom that a self-proclaimed virgin can muster, it was all I could do not to call him up and ask for his hand in marriage . . .

Like most Canadians, when I'm surfing the Internet, I have Canada's parliamentary affairs channel, CPAC, running in the background. I find I can work and think just a little bit more efficiently if I'm simultaneously entertained by the dull and dulcet tones of Peter MacKay or the shrieking wail of Anne McLellan.

Anyway, a few weeks back I happened to catch Don Boudria standing up in the House and I could tell he was hopping mad about the anti-same-sex-marriage crowd. Apparently they'd purchased one of Don's domain names and been playing silly buggers with it.

Don was upset that somebody stumbling across such a site would think that they were viewing an official Don Boudria website, and not a propaganda tool. Obviously Don thinks there are a lot of low-IQ voters out there Googling the hell out of Don Boudria. But I digress.

Don felt that this was a nasty below-the-belt tactic from the family values crowd. Well, the Conservative party wasn't going to have any of this bashing of the anti-SSM crowd so Jason Kenney jumped to his feet.

I love Jason. The honourable member from Calgary Southeast is the Conservative bright light who likes to point out that gays are allowed to get married—as long as they get married to members of the opposite sex! Jason Kenney: stupid and talking, my favourite combination in a politician. Needless to say, when Jason opens his mouth, I listen.

Long story short, Jason told Boudria it was his own fault for not registering his own domain name. I found myself agreeing with Jason on this; I mean, doesn't the Liberal party have access to a teenager who can advise them on this kind of stuff? I bet a guy like Jason does. Anyway, Jason was just getting started. I include here a transcript from Hansard for your edification:

Mr. Jason Kenney (Calgary Southeast, CPC): Mr. Speaker, the only additional element that the hon. member has brought to the Chair's attention relates to a matter which is in no way, shape or form within the purview of this House or your honour and it never has been, and hopefully never will be, that is to say, the registration of domain names on the World Wide Web.

I understand my hon. friend opposite is learned with respect to parliamentary procedure but I must infer from his remarks that he is stupefiedly ignorant about commercial practices on the Internet.

The Speaker: Honestly, the hon. member for Calgary Southeast need not suggest that any hon. member of this House is ignorant.

Mr. Jason Kenney: Mr. Speaker, of the Internet.

The Speaker: That does not make it better. He could say that he has perhaps missed the point or something. We do not need to use this kind of language. I would urge the hon. member to show some restraint.

Mr. Jason Kenney: Mr. Speaker, let me be clear. I did not mean ignorant in the pejorative sense but in an objective sense that the member apparently does not understand the process by which domain names are registered on the Internet.

While the Speaker was admonishing Jason for such unparliamentarily language as "ignorant," I started thinking: What are the chances that Jason Kenney is so stunned that he would call another MP ignorant for not having registered his domain name when he hadn't bothered to register his own?

Not a chance, I figured. I am not that lucky.

Turns out the chances were pretty good. Before he was down in his seat I was the proud owner of www.jasonkenney.org.

At first, the link drove web surfers to the Marxist-Leninist Party of Canada. I wanted something that screamed Jason. Then, in honour of Pride celebrations, www.jasonkenney.org was made to point to Egale Canada—"Equality for Gays and Lesbians Everywhere." My Canada includes Jason in a boa, surrounded by a dozen balloons and the Jason Kenney Dancers, vying for a best float prize in a Gay Pride parade.

Update. I still own jasonkenney.org. A few months back the domain name came up for renewal and I thought the Christian thing to do would be to call Jason Kenney and tell him he could have it. I came very close, but then I saw him on the news again, blathering on in that constantly incensed way of his, implying that anyone who is not on board with his vision of Canada is somehow anti-Canadian, and I just couldn't bring myself to do the right thing. So I renewed it until 2011.

Kenney desperately wants to be prime minister and spends half his time laying pipe behind the scenes to that end. Tragically, he believes that he has a good shot—which is why I figure the domain name just might come in handy someday. Until then, I will keep jasonkenney.org and continue to point it in places that I know will piss him off. Honestly—sometimes I believe that I'm still ten years old.

IN SEARCH OF THE TRUTH

The cliché is that in Question Period members of Parliament act like schoolchildren. This is not quite accurate; they act like the schoolchildren in *Lord of the Flies,* after the plane crash.

There are, however, certain lines that politicians cannot cross in the House of Commons. One of the biggest no-no's is suggesting a member of Parliament has lied. This is taken very seriously. If an MP accuses another MP of lying and doesn't immediately throw him or herself at the mercy of the Speaker and apologize profusely he'll be thrown out of the House until such time that an acceptable apology is issued.

It is a bit ironic that this rule exists, because playing loose with the truth is as second nature to politicians as leg humping is to a chihuahua.

It's also a fact of life that most politicians when asked will state unequivocally that their word is their bond. In this instance most of them are lying. In those rare instances when a politician develops a reputation for being honest, Canadians respond favourably.

This is why after being elected the Tories fell in love with the slogan "Promise made, promise kept." Like so many other utterances in the political universe, it turned out to be untrue.

IT USED TO BE CALLED LYING | OCT. 17, 2006

I'm happy to see that the Tories have finally unveiled their plan to fight climate change. The minister of the environment, Rona Ambrose, had been blathering on about her secret "made in Canada" plan for so long I was starting to worry that it didn't exist. But exist it does, and more importantly, the prime minister is on board. In fact Stephen Harper was so excited about this Tory environmental plan he gassed up the Challenger with 8,620 litres of jet fuel, put a couple of cabinet ministers in the back and flew all the way to Vancouver to be at Rona's side.

And what did Rona have to say? Absolutely nothing. This was the government's only announcement on the environment to date, and the minister of the environment wasn't allowed to say a single word. Harper didn't let her. You know, I think that's mean of the prime minister. Even Hef lets the bunnies say hello once in a while.

Harper did all the talking. He strode up to the podium with the majestic BC mountains behind him, and he made the big announcement. He announced that in the future there would be an announcement that involved consultation. And at that moment it became crystal clear to me that the prime minister of Canada thinks we're all idiots. In fact I've noticed lately that every time he addresses the Canadian people like that, he sounds less and less like a prime minister and more and more like a special ed teacher.

Of course there are some Tories who say he has no choice. He has to do all the talking, he's got to keep his cabinet quiet, because quite frankly his ministers are—how do I say this delicately—"not very good at their jobs."

They may have a point. The last time Rona was allowed to speak in public, she attacked the Liberals for wasting 100 million dollars on worthless emission credits. Which would be outrageous. Unfortunately for Rona, Greg Weston over at the *Toronto Sun* looked into it and her numbers were a little off—say, by 100 million dollars. Turns out Rona made the whole thing up to make the Liberals look bad and the Tories look good. You know, in the old days, under the Liberals, we called that lying. These days, under the Tories, it's called action on climate change.

UNTRUSTWORTHY | NOV. 7, 2006

Like most people, I find it completely unnerving when suddenly everyone in the room is talking about something that I can't even begin to understand. And when that happens to me, and it happens a lot, it usually involves math. So when Stephen Harper out of the blue put a bullet into those income trusts and all the seniors went crazy, I was completely lost. And then I realized, everything I know about income trusts I actually learned during the last election, and I learned from Stephen Harper.

I learned that it's the seniors more than any other group that invests in these things. And I heard Harper say over and over again that when he became prime minister, income trusts would be safe.

And you know what? I believed him. And so did a lot of seniors, apparently, because they went out and kept investing in the bloody things. And why not? Harper's entire shtick—something I do understand—is that you can believe what he says. The entire *raison d'être* of the Harper government is: You may not like what we do, but we do what we say; if we make a promise, you can take that to the bank. At a Harper rally you can't hear yourself think for all the Tories chanting "Promise made, promise kept" over and over like a herd of demented Moonies. Some of them get so excited that they start smacking themselves in the forehead while they chant it.

Well, thank God that's over. The next time you hear Stephen Harper say "Promise made, promise kept," you might want to back away, because if there is a God, the forecast calls for lightning. I'm sorry, Stephen. That's the chance you take when you mess with senior citizens and their hard-earned savings.

I know Harper has all sorts of excuses as to why he had to break this promise to the seniors, but you know what? I don't even care. I came to the conclusion a long time ago that there's only two reasons politicians break their promises: you've already voted for them, or you've already voted for them. Turns out some things never change.

TURNCOATS | FEB. 13, 2007

In Canada it used to be a very big deal when a member of Parliament crossed the floor. But these days it's becoming downright *de rigueur.* It was just the other day that Wajid Khan left the Liberals and joined the Tories—and now Garth Turner has come out as a Liberal. If this keeps up, they're going to have to kick-start every day in the House of Commons with a rousing game of "Red rover, red rover, send your whack jobs right over." Because let's face it, as far as big catches go, these guys are dubious at best.

You wouldn't know it, though. When Harper announced that Wajid had crossed the floor, he didn't act like he'd just snagged a car dealer from Toronto. He acted like the heavens had just opened and God himself had come down and declared that He was a Tory. In fact Harper was so grateful that he rewarded Wajid's treachery by making him the Conservative party's new international man of mystery. Now Wajid gets to travel around the world on the taxpayer's dime and write secret reports that nobody is ever allowed to see. They're so top secret that the prime minister won't even tell us whether they're written in pencil or pen. Let's face it, though—they're most likely written in crayon.

And then there's Garth Turner. After months of negotiations the Liberals have finally landed Garth. Or, depending on how you look at it—they came down with him. Now if I were Dion, I would have to ask myself, do I want Garth Turner? Because with Garth it's not a question of whether he's a Tory or a Liberal—it's a question of whether he's a maverick or a renegade. Which is fine if you're looking for someone to play the lead in a cheesy cop show, but not if you're looking for someone to sit in your caucus.

In politics, in the party system, the one thing that everyone agrees on is this: the most important attribute is loyalty. And these guys have none. Yet by landing them, both leaders are claiming a massive moral victory, all the while ignoring the fact that when you bring someone into your party from purgatory, more often then not it leads to hell.

SAVVY TEACHERS' PLAN

JAN. 9, 2004

I think all of us in Canada, somewhere along the line, had a special teacher who helped us out along the way, who gave us a special nudge in the right direction. Or so I've read.

And when we think "teacher," many words and phrases come to mind, though "business savvy" is probably well down on the list. But in fact Canada's teachers are very savvy. Teachers' pension plans in this country are some of the biggest and most powerful in

Canada, the most successful of them all being the Ontario Teachers' Pension Plan.

Why are their plans so successful? Because teachers invest in the kids. They know, for example, that for many children these days the best part of waking up is Ritalin with their cereal. It only makes sense that Ontario teachers have over $22 million invested in the makers of Ritalin. Which is why if a teacher thinks your kid should be on Ritalin, that's not a coincidence—that's what they call "synergy."

Teachers are all about synergy. And that is why a few years back Ontario's teachers bought a company called Cadillac Fairview, one of largest owners of shopping malls in all of North America.

That is savvy. Once you know that the teachers actually own the malls, it's easier to understand their negotiation methods. When teachers work to rule, the kids go to the mall. Volleyball may be cancelled, but the food court is still open.

Teachers realize, though, that not all children want to play by the rules. They don't want to eat their Ritalin and hang out in the food court. Some kids, the bad kids, like to hang out *outside* the mall and smoke cigarettes. And that is why the Ontario Teachers' Pension Plan has over 64 million dollars invested in the tobacco industry.

Now I'm not saying teachers think its okay for young people to smoke, just that with 64 million dollars on the line they've got to be hoping that young people *will* smoke. Especially the girls, because they think they look fat.

And in all fairness, the Ontario Teachers' Pension Plan website points out that $40 million of that money is invested in the Phillip Morris tobacco company, which considers itself an industry leader in convincing young people to butt out.

So kids, if tomorrow in school your teacher asks you why you don't have your homework done, you can say, "You know miss, or sir, I don't have my homework done because I was watching TV. But I learned a very important lesson. I learned that teachers are savvy. And apparently you have a piece of everything, and are deserving of our respect. Much like the well-loved fictional character Tony Soprano."

So in conclusion, I implore every child in Canada to look at their teachers with new respect. Because while the bell may ring at 2:45 p.m., your teachers are always with you. In every mall you hang out in, in every Ritalin you swallow, and in every cigarette you smoke.

Update: The Ontario Teachers' Pension Plan still has shares in Novartis, the maker of Ritalin and Altria, the parent company of Philip Morris International. We asked the OTPP to comment and a spokesperson said: "By law, public pension plans cannot screen investments on the sole basis of social, environmental, political, or other non-financial criteria. The Ontario Teachers' Pension Plan has a responsibility to make investment decisions that are in plan members' best financial interests after carefully considering all the factors that could impact a company's long-term performance. If plan members want a social investment screen for the plan's investment, they must first decide which investments are acceptable, and then get the Ontario government—the other plan sponsor—to change the law."

MY NEWFOUNDLAND, RIGHT OR WRONGED

John Crosbie, the face and voice of Newfoundland politics for many a decade, never saw a microphone he didn't like and never opened up without a joke. One of his favourites was, how do you spot the Newfoundlanders in Heaven? They're the ones who want to go home.

It's funny because it's true.

PAUL'S NEW DEAL | NOV. 8, 2004

I can remember being in junior high when they wheeled in TV sets so that we could watch as Brian Peckford, the premier of Newfoundland, held up a beaker of oil and announced that the days of being a have-not province would soon be over.

The entire class burst into laughter. Because we knew what we were: we were the poorest province in Canada. And if you ever forgot that, all you had to do was wait five minutes and someone would remind you. We also knew that if there was ever any money in this offshore oil racket, somehow Newfoundland would get ripped off.

And now, twenty-odd years and five premiers later, still no deal.

We had a deal, we had a really good deal—we had a deal with Paul Martin. In the middle of the last campaign, Martin stood up and said that Newfoundland should be able to receive 100 per cent of its oil revenues, no ifs, ands or buts. And then, as if the gods of cruelty were watching, it was snatched away in about as much time as it took for Newfoundland to vote Liberal. After which, the people at the Department of Finance started to hear rumours that maybe Newfoundland wouldn't be so poor all of a sudden, and panicked.

And now there's a new deal: Newfoundland gets to keep its profits, but only as long as it remains poorer than Ontario. Apparently the notion that the poor, ignorant Newfoundlanders could some day be as good as the crowd in Ontario is so offensive that safeguards have to be built in to ensure that this never happens.

Newfoundland is supposed to go along with this? Mr. Martin, I don't know much, but I know this: that is never going to happen. Because if stubborn paid money, Newfoundland would be rich.

A deal is a deal. Newfoundlanders knows that. We've seen enough bad ones to last a lifetime.

DANNY FOR LEADER | APR. 11, 2006

The 39th Parliament has been up and running for a week, and it is not what I expected. What amazes me about watching Prime Minister Harper in action is just how cocky the guy is. And he's not cocky because he thinks he's so good. He's cocky because when he looks at all the people that want to lead the Liberal party, he feels invincible.

If you're a Liberal, this is a very bad sign. The Liberals can have all the namby-pamby conversations they want about what Liberal qualities they need in a leader, but what they should really be asking themselves is one question only: Who will put the fear of God into Stephen Harper?

I've looked at the list of candidates, and the choice is obvious. Danny Williams for leader of the Liberals.

I know the guy is not a Liberal. But people are starting to change parties like they change pants. And I know the guy's got a job. He's the premier of Newfoundland. Doesn't matter, the boss is very organized. He can do two jobs. Actually, three jobs. Because he should also be the premier of Alberta.

And I would like to say that he should have these jobs because he's the only one who's qualified, but that's not it. It's that when you look around the political landscape, he's the only guy with a vision. People actually know what he stands for, and in Liberal circles that would make him unique. Plus, he has the added bonus of being able to take a cocky guy like Stephen Harper and turn him into a whimpering simp before breakfast. That's what the Liberal party needs, and it doesn't have it. So if I were them, I'd keep looking, or the party might be over.

NOT ALBERTA | OCT. 24, 2006

Depending on who you ask, this week Newfoundland picked a fight with Ottawa or Ottawa picked a fight with Newfoundland.

I have no idea who threw the first punch, but I know this: right now the relationship between Stephen Harper and Danny Williams is about as friendly as the one between Paul McCartney and Heather Mills. I wouldn't be surprised if at any minute Danny went totally Paul McCartney on us and tried to stab Harper in the leg with a broken wine glass.

Mind you, to hear Harper's people tell it, the prime minister has had a huge triumph. He had the courage to fly down to Newfoundland and give Danny a smack that sent a message to everyone in Atlantic Canada.

Danny wants something called fallow field legislation, and Harper doesn't want him to have it. Danny wants to be able to tell oil companies that if they discover oil in Newfoundland, they've got to use it or they lose it, because as it stands now, if they discover oil, they don't have to develop it at all. They can sit on that oil forever like it's some sort of guaranteed RRSP.

This is an epic struggle. This is the people of Atlantic Canada versus oil companies in Houston. And I ask you, do you think anyone on God's green earth believes that Steven Harper's going to side with Atlantic Canada on this one? And anyway, where does Danny get off thinking Newfoundland, of all places, can have fallow field legislation? Where the hell does Danny think he is? Alberta?

Maybe he does. Because you know what? They've got it in Alberta. In Alberta, if you discover oil, you've got five years to develop it, after which the Province tells you to get out of the way while they bring in someone who will. But of course, that's Alberta. And in Stephen Harper's Canada, Atlantic Canada and Alberta are treated very differently.

As it stands now, oil companies in Alberta make money by finding oil and then producing oil, but they can make money in Newfoundland by finding oil and producing nothing.

And unfortunately, "nothing for Newfoundland" is a principle Stephen Harper will fight for.

MERCER: These things go up the side of cliffs.

WILLIAMS: I think the real practical application for me would be if I could get this thing to go up the side of the Peace Tower. Be kind of a King Kong kind of thing, you know.

Later, during an extremely bumpy ride . . .

WILLIAMS: I'd like to have Steve here in the Jeep with me for this one.

MERCER: And by Steve you mean our prime minister?

WILLIAMS: I do.

OFF-ROAD WITH DANNY WILLIAMS

A 4 x 4, Seal Cove, Newfoundland and Labrador. Broadcast Oct. 23, 2007

MERCER: He doesn't like being called Steve.

WILLIAMS: Is that right? I never knew that. Are you serious? It's his name.

THE IGGY ENIGMA

Poor Michael Ignatieff. All the man wanted to do was return to Canada, become a cabinet minister in Paul Martin's government and then, after a few years, assume his rightful position as king of the Dominion of Canada. Of course, when he made this plan how could he have known that Martin and the Liberal party were destined for defeat? Well, he could have read it in a newspaper, I suppose, but the sad reality is that most newsstands in America do not carry either *The Globe and Mail* or the *National Post*. Iggy was out there in the big, bad world flying on nothing but his instincts.

So Iggy returned to Canada as planned and no sooner had he landed and got himself elected in the cozy safe Liberal riding of Etobicoke Lakeshore than the Liberals were defeated and Iggy had no choice but to run for the leadership of the party . . .

GLAD YOU COULD MAKE IT | APR. 4, 2006

The Liberal leadership race got a little more interesting this week when Michael Ignatieff, or Iggy, as his friends call him, finally made it pretty much official that he wants the top job. And personally, I like the cut of his jib.

For starters, he's a worker bee. You can't take that away from the man. Every time you turn around, there's Iggy, writing another speech, making another presentation on the subject of torture. I admire anyone who has a hobby. There are a couple of nervous Nellies out there who find it a little disconcerting that the so-called saviour of the Liberal party constantly has to clarify whether or not he's obsessed with putting electrodes on people's genitals. I say, what odds, bring it on, it might even brighten up the convention. I mean, God knows what Iggy's got planned for those tense couple of hours between the second and third ballots.

Also, I admire anyone who can take an unpopular position and stick with it. Iggy is pretty much the only Liberal in Canada who believes Chrétien was wrong in keeping Canada out of the war in Iraq. But see, that's Iggy for you. Iggy is not handicapped by that whole Canadian point of view thing. He hasn't lived in Canada in thirty years. Which is fine by me. You have to go where the work is. And I'm sure he's got people who explain to him all that boring old Canadian stuff like who Don Cherry is or what the hell's a Nunavut. That doesn't matter, because Iggy is an ideas man and he's got an idea that he should be our prime minister. And I say, more power to him, nice of him to pop in and give it a whirl.

HYPOTHETICALLY SPEAKING | SEPT. 6, 2006

I was encouraged to read that Michael Ignatieff will not accept any questions from the media that are "anticipatory hypotheticals." I'm glad he made this clear, because I hope to interview him on the show this year, and I appreciate the heads-up. Truth is, I like Iggy. It's just that sometimes I don't know what in the hell he's talking about. I thought all hypotheticals were anticipatory. I am so stupid sometimes. I Googled the phrase "anticipatory hypothetical" and there are only seven known uses out there. The term pops up on a website called indiansex.com, and it's also used in an essay written by some dude in Iowa who believes that robots have taken over the world.

SMARTEST GUY IN THE ROOM | SEPT. 20, 2006

In the media Ignatieff is usually described as "current front-runner." Soon that will make way for "former front-runner," and eventually Ignatieff will simply be called "disappointed." This was not the way this was supposed to play out.

Iggy's problem is not the number of delegates he has or his support in the Liberal caucus. He's got a healthy pile of those folks in his pocket. His problem is that while delegates may be political junkies, they work and walk among civilians. Part of the job of a delegate is to constantly bore the hell out of everyone at the office talking about this leadership race. And as the leadership slowly makes it onto the civilian radar, more and more civilians are asking their delegate friends why the hell they think Michael Ignatieff is electable.

Right now there are a lot of confirmed Iggy supporters who are starting to wonder whether or not they have backed the wrong horse.

Some people have suggested that Canadians aren't warming to Iggy because of his intellectual credentials. I don't buy this. Canadians don't mind that Ignatieff is the smartest guy in the room; what bugs us is that he acts like it. We can't relate to a guy like that. Personally, I'm happy if I'm the smartest guy in the elevator.

To be fair, though, acting like you're the smartest guy in the room is probably an occupational hazard that comes with being a Harvard professor. And this alone isn't fatal; in fact it's pretty common. Our current prime minister also thinks he's the smartest guy in the room—although when you consider the type of room Harper usually finds himself in, you can hardly blame him. When Harper exits a caucus meeting, it's not entirely clear if the title "smartest guy in the room" immediately shifts to his parliamentary secretary or to the jade plant.

My gut feeling that suddenly this is Rae's race is hardly scientific. There are still some people who think Iggy can take this sucker on the first ballot, and really the opinion of a non-delegate like me watching at home on the couch is entirely irrelevant.

Also, in the spirit of full disclosure I have to admit that there were times during the debate when I was not entirely awake; in fact, I think I nodded off a few times. I was, like so many other Canadians, simply killing time on a Sunday evening staring at the TV with a beer between my knees—and from that perspective Bob Rae is now the guy to beat.

FROM THE TELEPROMPTER OF MICHAEL IGNATIEFF | OCT. 16, 2006

Ladies and gentlemen, honoured guests, protester standing silently at the back of the room with a bag on his head, thank you for coming here today.

It has been almost one year now since I made the difficult decision to immigrate to Canada and run for the leadership of the Liberal Party of Canada. Since that time I have taken clear positions on difficult issues and I have taken difficult positions on clear issues. Unfortunately, many people do not seem to understand what I am talking about. If anyone is at fault here it is me; please bear with me, Canada, I am used to teaching the advanced class.

I asked you to come here today so that I might clarify my statements concerning an earlier clarification about a statement I may or may not have meant to make.

As you may know, earlier this year my summer vacation overseas was interrupted by a small war between Israel and Lebanon. The fact that my vacation was interrupted by this war is not in doubt. I have made myself unequivocally clear about this point.

After returning to Canada, I stated during a frank discussion about the war that I was not losing sleep over civilian deaths in Lebanon. Some people wrongly interpreted this to mean that I was not losing sleep over civilian deaths in Lebanon. What I should have said at the time was this: I am not losing sleep over civilian deaths in Lebanon because I suffer from hysterical narcolepsy, a rare neurological disorder. Because of this condition it is not just civilian deaths that I sleep through, but sometimes entire movies and even midair turbulence. I hope that by admitting this I will not only clear up an unfortunate misunderstanding but also help the other half dozen of my fellow Americans who suffer from this disorder. For too long we have suffered in silence.

Please visit www.hystericalnarcolepsy.org and learn more about this condition. Hysterical narcolepsy—the confusion is real.

Let us now deal with the elephant in the room. While campaigning in Quebec I stated that Israel was guilty of war crimes. Please know I made these comments in French and never intended them to be heard by English voters.

Clearly everything I have read about the two solitudes is a fallacy. I now believe that the bridge between French and English Canada is the fluently bilingual Toronto Jew. In fact I would like to take a moment and speak directly to the good men and women of the Holy Blossom temple in Toronto. I say to you, my Jewish friends—join me! It's Iggy time! (*Pause for applause*)

Please, please sit. There is more! (*Wave finger*)

In an effort to keep this story in the media during the coming weeks, I have decided to visit Israel for myself. I think you will agree that the crucial last days of a leadership race is the perfect time for a candidate to leave Canada.

The purpose of this trip will be twofold. Not only will I be able to analyze and solve the Israel-Lebanon issue, but I have also requested that the Canada-Israel Committee, which is sponsoring this trip, arrange a stopover in Paris on the way back so I can get a good meal. I have been in Canada for months now and, my friends, I am getting antsy. (*Chuckle kindly*)

When I return from my pilgrimage to the Holy Land, I think you will see a refreshed and tanned Michael Ignatieff, one who is ready to tackle the job of running Canada for all of you. And when I say you, I mean the fishers, the farmers and the Mennonites who make this country strong.

Speaking of Canada, recently a little boy in Canada's countryside asked me a very intriguing question. "Sir," he said, "why do you want to run all of Canada?"

I will tell you now what I told him then.

Canada is in my osseous tissue! (*Pause for applause*)

Like you, I care about Canadian values and Canadian pastimes. I know what it's like to clear one's mind and enjoy the thrust and parry that is found in an exciting ice hockey game. In fact, I don't mind admitting that I have always been, since the 1968 Trudeau leadership campaign in which I was a delegate, a supporter of the Toronto Maple Leafs. My support for the Leafs is something that is pure and true and can never be taken away from me. If there is a political price to pay for such an admission, I readily accept it. *Mesdames et Messieurs, j'aime les Canadiens. Les Leafs de Toronto sont gay! Vive les Sens! Vive les Sens libre!*

I want to thank you for your time today, ladies and gentlemen. And on a personal note, I would like to thank the numerous people who have sent me letters and cards encouraging me during these recent dark, gaffe-riddled days of the campaign. But let me tell you this. When I embarked on this adventure I knew it would not be easy. And when the going gets tough, when I think I cannot bear another conversation with another Canadian or another question about Bob Rae, I simply close my eyes and think of that great Canadian Terry Fox. And it is that image of Terry Fox courageously circling the globe in his wheelchair that gives me the courage to move forward.

(*Pause for really,* really *big round of applause*)

Thank you for your support.

I embrace you!

THAT OTHER GUY (II)

RAE OF HOPE | SEPT. 20, 2006

I remember exactly where I was the moment I heard that Bob Rae wanted to be leader of the Liberal party. It's one of those seared-in-the-memory thingies, like recalling where you were when the *Challenger* blew up or you heard Stockwell Day is straight.

Bob Rae wanting to be Liberal leader seemed so bizarre I figured it was just a matter of time before he'd be on TV revealing the tragic results of the CAT scan.

Nothing against Rae, of course—I'm sure he means well—it's just that his record as NDP premier of Ontario will never go away. It's like herpes.

But watching the debate in Vancouver I realized that my initial reaction was way off. Believe it or not, Bob Rae has the big mo. Standing up there on the stage in front of all those Liberals, Bob Rae looked like a prime minister and Michael Ignatieff looked like he was digesting a bag of California spinach.

FISHING WITH BOB RAE

Killarney Provincial Park.
Broadcast Oct. 10, 2006

RAE: I want to take the government away from being ideological . . . I think you've got to take care of people. I think you've got to have a government that provides some leadership that's pragmatic, that's thoughtful, that's not going to be based on these crappy, right-wing ideologies.

MERCER: Can you say that again, but in a funny way?

THE TRIALS OF LORD BLACK

Finding myself rooting for Conrad Black is way up there on the list of things I never imagined I could or would do. But when push came to shove and his Lordship faced his accusers in Chicago I found myself rooting for the home team. Because despite his bizarre citizenship status, I still think of the guy as ours.

In the midst of his legal troubles he agreed to appear on the show and wax both figuratively and literally on the Canadian maple leaf. He did a great job at both.

At the time he was not allowed to leave the United States, so we arranged to shoot the segment at his home in Palm Beach, Florida. The day I spent with him there still resonates as one of the most surreal experiences of my life. And while he was certainly a charming and pleasant enough host, he struck me as every inch a prisoner, albeit in his own home.

Today, of course, he is a true prisoner, in a very ugly American prison.

I look forward to the day when he can walk out of that place, return to his home in Canada and resume his rightful place as the Canadian who bugs us more than any other.

Good luck on an early release, Connie!

TAKE BACK BLACK | MAR. 5, 2004

I like to watch the high and almighty fall as much as anyone, but watching Conrad Black suffer is just too painful. Every time they run his picture in the paper, the man looks like he's aged fifteen years. He looks like Gollum now.

One minute he's a multi-millionaire press baron and the next he's in danger of losing it all, his money and his reputation. He's said himself that this turn of events has made him a social pariah. And you know what that means. All the other lords are laughing and calling him names. They're not letting poor Conrad join any lord and lady games, like fox hunting and fancy-dress parties and stuff.

What are we as a nation going to do about it? Because from what I've heard it's very expensive to live in London, even if you're just a normal person. If you're a flat broke social leper, it must be almost impossible. He'll have no other choice but to totally reinvent himself. He'll have to become the wacky lord who sits in the pub and swallows pickled eggs for pints. And we don't want that. Not really.

So I propose that we take back Conrad Black. Sure he gave up his Canadian citizenship so he could become a lord, but that's all in the past now. The guy was born here, he made his fortune here, he became the giant poncy tool he is today here. The least we can do is offer him the benefit of the social safety net.

And if he has to go on welfare until he gets back on his feet, so be it. That's why we pay taxes, to help those less fortunate than us.

. . . **AND NEVER LET HIM FORGET IT** | OCT. 3, 2006

When I saw the headline in the newspaper I swear to God I heard angels sing. *"Conrad Black wants Canadian citizenship back."* Cue the trumpets—it just doesn't get much better than this.

Seeing that headline made me so excited, I couldn't even read the bloody story. I picked up the paper and brought it home like it was a box of chocolates. I didn't even glance at the first sentence until everything was perfect. The coffee was brewed, my feet were up, the pillow behind my neck was just so. This was a moment to be savoured.

And it was a great moment. As I read that story, I don't think I ever felt more Canadian, because I knew that for perhaps the first time in our nation's history, everyone in Canada was on the same page. We were united. We were gloating as one.

And what a story—Conrad Black, a man who once had more than any of us could ever imagine, gladly gave up the one thing we all share and hold dear: a Canadian citizenship. And why? So he could go to Britain and become

Lord Black of Crossdresser. And now, after telling the entire country to shove it, he wants back in.

I have to admit, the idea of Conrad Black down at the immigration office stuck in the back of a line behind some poor Somali dude with a bullet in his leg fills my heart with joy. The *Schadenfreude* is on bust here. Conrad is basically at the front door of Canada saying to every one of us, "I'm sorry, baby, I didn't mean it: Let me back in the house."

And like so many Canadians, part of me wants to barricade the door, run up the stairs and start pouring hot bubbly oil out of the top window all over his little lord costume—the red one with the big white fur neck.

But unfortunately, that's not the Canadian way. I hate to say it, but I think we have to take the high road. We shouldn't humiliate the guy any more, no matter how much we want to. Bottom line is, it's fun to "kick up," but it's unseemly to kick a guy when he's down. Granted, Conrad Black's version of being down is slightly different than for the rest of us. His assets are frozen and he must somehow get by on a measly $45,000 a month. There are rumours he might sell the Bentley.

And besides, seeing Conrad fighting for his life in the American courts makes me root for the guy. As it stands now, he insists he will fight to the death in court and that there will be no plea bargain. He has even described himself, without a hint of irony, as a "freedom fighter." Will future generations of university students and skateboarders take down the pictures of Che Guevara and replace them with woodcut prints of Lord Black?

Now just to be clear, I'm not suggesting Conrad should get special treatment—I'm suggesting he should be treated like a Canadian.

Because regardless of what was said, or what papers were signed in the heat of the moment, that's exactly what he is. Yes, he denied us, yes, we all heard the cock crow, but that had more to do with his getting into a peeing match with Jean Chrétien than anything else. That was then, this is now. I suggest we have to do the right thing, the Canadian thing, and give him the citizenship back—and then, being Canadian, we never ever let him forget it. We lord it over the lord forever. Amen.

WAXING LYRICAL WITH CONRAD BLACK

At his Florida residence.
Broadcast Oct. 2, 2007

LORD BLACK: A perfectly waxed maple leaf . . . a great solace to everyone, and especially to those who, for complicated reasons, can't, at first hand, observe the changing of the seasons this autumn in Canada.

WOULD ALL THE PEOPLE WITH A KNIGHTHOOD PLEASE SHUT UP

JUNE 22, 2005

I know I'm cynical about these things, but when Bob Geldof tells Canada's prime minister to stay at home and skip the G8 summit, are we not supposed to laugh our asses off? Did a memo go out saying that aging rock stars are setting the agenda at the G8 now? Would the world be a better place if the Bob Geldofs were running it?

Don't get me wrong. It's not that I don't think people like Sir Bob have a place on the world stage. If I was to hold an international symposium on getting off junk or the perils of autoerotic asphyxiation, I would expect a healthy number of rock stars with royal titles to take part.

Something tells me that Sir Bob is a little bitter about Bono getting too much attention.

NATIONS WITHIN OUR NATION

In this section I take a look around the Canadian mosaic, which still just about includes Quebec but unfortunately hasn't yet embraced the Turks and Caicos.

A while ago the Quebec bar association gave an award to the Right Honourable Brian Mulroney for his work in convincing Stephen Harper to recognize the Québécois as a nation. There are surely many more Harper-related accolades coming Mulroney's way. At some point in the near future Mulroney will have to be honoured for convincing Stephen Harper not only to act like him but to become him.

Part of the fun of watching Harper in action has been seeing this metamorphosis take place. Stephen Harper, the one-time Western reformer and personal advocate of small government is now the Quebec-focused big-spending prime minister who is allergic to personal income tax cuts. The more things change, the more they stay the same.

CLIMATE CHANGE | JAN. 23, 2004

I love Canada as much as the next guy. I've always believed that if you were born in Canada, you had won the lotto. But that said, at this time of the year even the most dyed-in-the-wool Canadian can be forgiven for wondering why anyone in their right mind would want to live in a frozen hellhole like this. We all have our weak moments.

But now the solution is here. It's been suggested recently that perhaps the Turks and Caicos, a little bit of Caribbean paradise, just might want to become a Canadian province or territory.

Now, this is not a new idea. In fact, do you know who came up with it? Robert Borden, in 1917. In typical Parliament Hill fashion, good ideas sometimes take about a hundred years to get recognized. But the amazing thing about this proposal is that it's doable.

There are only about twenty thousand citizens in the Turks and Caicos. Population-wise, this is like picking up a small Canadian town, with sunshine and beaches. And yes, they would have to be given Canadian-style health care, but come on—how much does it cost to tell twenty thousand people they have to wait six months for a CAT scan?

Paul Martin should jump at this. How many prime

ministers get to add another province? Come on, Paul. George Bush is attempting to inspire Americans with a vision of putting an American on the surface of Mars. Shag that. You want to inspire Canadians, give them a vision of parking their ass on a beach for week. Go for it, Paul. My Canada includes a forty-below windchill factor—but my Canada also includes the Turks and Caicos.

LAST CHANCE TO VOTE | NOV. 1, 2005

Every now and again it's good for all of us to sit back and take stock of where we have been and where we are going. Or at least that's the advice of people who are far smarter than I am.

It's been just over ten years since Quebec went to the polls and voted in the last referendum. Ten years since we as a nation came together, sat around on our couches, ate chips and watched as the country teetered on the brink of total destruction. And of course since then, the greatest minds and the greatest leaders a nation could muster have worked together and done their best to ensure that Canada is even more screwed up now than it was back then.

Ten years ago, if you drove around Calgary, the bumper stickers said, "The West Wants In"; now they say "The West Wants Out." Ask the people why and they'll blame the East, and by the East they are referring to Ontario. This drives me nuts, because if you look at a map, Ontario's really more in the middle. The East is that other part of Canada, where the only way they can get anyone to pay attention to them is to pull the Maple Leaf down off the flagpoles.

And Quebec—cripes, if you're a federalist in Quebec, you couldn't get elected as a prostate examiner. And you can't really blame the bloody Québécois. What federalists are they supposed to vote for? The Liberals are criminals, and the Tories don't even speak French.

Imagine if you were ten years old on referendum night. That means you're twenty now and your entire life experience as a citizen of Canada has been witnessing a nation in crisis management. It's like we get off on it or something.

And only 38 per cent of twenty-year-olds voted in the last election.

We know now that there's going to be another election in Canada very soon. Please, if you're under twenty, do us a favour: this time get off the couch and vote. Because if you leave it to the rest of us, it might just be your last chance.

LOSING AT CHESS | NOV. 28, 2006

You have to hand it to Stephen Harper—the man is on a roll.

The Tories like to say that Harper is good at his job because above all else, he is a master chess player. In one bold move, he stood up in the House of Commons, he embarrassed the Bloc and he protected his own seats in Quebec. And all he had to do was table a simple motion that says from now on, the government of Canada recognizes that the Québécois form a nation inside a nation.

So all you kids in grade three can forget what you just learned about Canada being ten provinces and three territories. We are now nine provinces, three territories and a nation inside a nation.

When you write this down, kids, you might want to use a pencil. Because there's going to be a lot more nations to learn about. Take the Cree in Quebec. Clearly they're a nation. Well actually, they're a nation inside a nation inside a nation. Imagine you are a Cree person who is gay, who cheers for the Blue Jays and who lives in Montreal. You'd be a member of the Cree nation, you'd hang out in the Queer nation, you'd cheer along with the rest of the Blue Jays nation and you'd live in the Quebec nation, which just happened to be inside the Canadian nation.

Yes, clearly Harper is a great strategist. But obviously he did not grow up in a huge family. Because if he did, he would know that, sure, some kids get away with more than others, some kids even get special treatment, but there is not a hope in hell that Mom will ever stand up and recognize one child as her favourite. No special status. And why? Because Mom knows that if she ever put that in writing, say, in a birthday card, it's exactly the type of thing that could destroy the entire works.

So whip-de-do-da-day, Stephen Harper plays a mean

game of chess. But I hope he realizes Canada is not a board game but a nation. And we only have one to lose.

SAME-SEX THURSDAY | DEC. 6, 2006

The debate over same-sex marriage is back. I see this as a positive development. Where did Canadians get the idea that once a minority's rights are defined they are somehow set in stone? It's time Canadians woke up and realized those days are long gone. This is an era of reflection.

Sure the Charter looks nice hanging on a wall, but the fact is, it grants far too many rights that are contrary to the deeply held personal views of many chubby white guys.

I hear rumours that the Conservatives plan on devoting every Thursday in the House of Commons to more votes on minority rights. Their list of motions so far includes debates on whether the Chinese should be allowed to drive, whether women should be allowed to vote and whether turbans should be allowed in elevators that travel more than sixteen floors.

In order to ensure that all minorities are targeted equally, the Conservatives have come up with an ingenious way of creating motions.

This year, in lieu of a Secret Santa exchange, every Tory has to write on a slip of paper the name of a minority that bugs them. On the back of the slip they must write a so-called "right we all enjoy." The slips will be mixed up and placed in a gorgeous festive ballot box decorated by John Baird for the occasion. At this year's Christmas party, each member will be blindfolded and asked to draw a slip of paper out of the box. That slip of paper is their own present and Canada's too. Imagine the hilarity that will ensue when Justice Minister Vic Toews stands up and says, "This year my Christmas gift is a motion to debate whether Hindus can own property in New Brunswick."

I can hear the laughter from here.

DOG OF A BLOG

MAY 30, 2007

The Conservative party has launched a website dedicated to bringing Canadians something called "Kyoto's Blog." This is a scathing piece of satire, presented as if it had been written by Stéphane Dion's dog. The premise alone is hysterical. Think about it. Dogs can't write and yet this dog apparently has a blog! Can you imagine how funny it would be to see a dog typing on a computer? I wish I'd had this idea.

From a show-business perspective it's interesting that Prime Minister Harper is making the blog available in both official languages. This is cutting edge and very risky because comedy in English generally doesn't translate well into French, especially this kind. And by "this kind" I mean the "Let's make the French look stupid because they are French" kind.

In this official Conservative party blog, Kyoto the dog likes to quote his "master" Stéphane Dion, and of course Dion speaks in broken English. According to the dog, no matter what is said to Dion he reacts by saying, "You don't know what you speak about!" The dumb Frenchie can't speak English! Dion is not a leader because English is his second language and he makes mistakes!

Kyoto also says really funny things, like "Time for bed. I'll dream about France. Stéphane tells me we will move back one day."

Dion was born in Quebec and has lived most of his life in Canada, but his mother is from France. I think the Conservatives' idea is that if people in English Canada keep being told that Dion is from France they will eventually believe it and he will become even more unpopular. There is comedy for you: Stéphane Dion's mother is an immigrant! An immigrant's son wants to be prime minister!

While I'm sure this kills inside the Conservative caucus, I'm not so sure it will elicit the same guffaws in Quebec—but hey, I have been wrong before.

BULLIES

Parliament is populated with bullies. The Tories' front man on a dozen issues, John Baird, loves nothing more than to stand up in the house and bully an opposing member with the glee of a neglected thirteen-year-old.

Watching bullies in the House—and every party has them—you can't help but think they must be part of this "cycle of abuse" we hear so much about. Look at the MPs who get in the most trouble for unparliamentary behaviour—MPs like Pierre Poilievre. Aren't they really yelling and screaming at some demons from a playground past? This is purely a guess, but I bet a guy like Pierre didn't have much of an opportunity to bully kids when he was in junior high and so when he gives people the finger in the House of Commons, he's just making up for lost time. Unfortunately, it works. In the House of Commons he who yells the loudest and is the most demeaning often wins.

HOUSE PARTY | NOV. 15, 2004

I was in Ottawa last week. I went up to the House of Commons, I sat up in the gallery and I watched Question Period live in all its glory.

The one thing you can always rely on about Question Period is this: no matter how badly behaved the members were on your last visit, things will have gotten way worse.

Question Period now is like your grade-seven class if your teacher had left you alone for five minutes to go out for a smoke and never returned. Any pretence of civility has left the building. When John Efford, the minister of natural resources, stands up to answer a question, nobody can hear a word the man is saying, because the minute he opens his mouth, Stephen Harper leads the entire opposition in a chorus of "Na na na na, na na na na, hey hey-eh, goodbye." They're singing songs on the floor of the House of Commons. And it's very effective. Efford looks like he's gonna burst into tears any minute.

There's so much racket in there that if you closed your eyes you'd swear you were at a hockey game. It's as if Tourette's syndrome suddenly became airborne, but only inside of Parliament.

I like it.

Nothing got accomplished. But the prime minister and his ministers had no choice but to sit there and take every single question and every single insult. Not a bad system, really, but one that has to be seen to be believed. Every Canadian should look in on Question Period once before they die, if for no other reason than to have their worst suspicions confirmed. And their best ones as well. Believe me, it's worth the price of admission—which, like Canada, is absolutely free.

YOU'LL PAY FOR THIS | MAR. 7, 2006

What a week for Ralph Klein. After years of threatening to unleash it upon the nation, Ralph has finally unveiled his Third Way Health Care Plan. Not to be confused of course with his Three Ways to Embarrass Yourself Plan, which he also unveiled this week.

Ralph's health care plan is pretty straightforward. Basically, if you're on a waiting list for a new hip, you should be able to slap down your gold card, pay twelve grand and go to the front of the line. If you don't have twelve grand, you go to the back of the line. Thanks, Ralph.

If you're the type of person who can pay for a hip, you've always had that option. It's not the third way, it's the American way. You don't call Ralph, you call Air Canada. You go to Chicago, you give them twelve grand, they'll give you a new hip by Friday. If you ask nice, they might even give you a boob job.

But the advantage of Ralph's way is that not only does it make it easier for people with money, it makes it harder for people without money. In Ralph's world, that's a bonus.

Now before you get upset that I'm implying that Ralph is some sort of out-of-control bully, it should be pointed out that this week, while trying to sell this plan, Mr. Threeway became so upset he literally threw a book at a seventeen-year-old girl who works as a page in the Alberta legislature.

I ask you, Canada, who in the hell does this? I mean, come on, Ralph, you're a grown man. You're the size of a frigging bull, for God's sakes, and you're throwing things at a teenage girl whose job it is to pass you things. If you did that in grade eight, you'd be sent home.

You'd be told to pack your books and your kirpan and go the hell home out of it.

So what happens to Ralph? Nothing. He apologizes for the umpteenth time and then goes about his business of promoting the third way. Or, as Ralph would say, "Make it a triple."

EDUCATING RONA | JAN. 9, 2007

Poor old Rona Ambrose, eh? The woman becomes the minister of the environment in a government that says right off the top that the environment is not a priority; she does exactly what she's told, which is basically nothing; and then she gets the slap for it.

But make no mistake, the rise and fall of Rona Ambrose says very little about Rona's abilities, and everything about the prime minister. Because Stephen Harper, he made it clear from day one. He's the head coach here. He put Rona in the game, he called the play, it went badly, she took the blame.

But of course, for Harper, a blaming wasn't good enough. He also arranged for her to have a good old-fashioned shaming. The one thing you can say about the Harper government is this: leaks never happen. If there is a leak, it is always intentional. So when word got out that poor old Rona was on deathwatch you can be guaranteed that the news came directly from head office. And Harper, he got to sit back over the holidays for five weeks, put up his feet and read two thousand articles that said Rona was about to be fired for total incompetence.

You know, this represents a new style in Canadian politics. Chrétien, Mulroney, they would crawl over broken glass to protect a cabinet minister. Whereas Harper takes a different approach. He takes the angry, disappointed dad-with-a-penchant-for-lashing-out approach.

Thanks to what happened to Rona, every single cabinet minister got the message loud and clear. When things go well, Dad takes the credit; when things go bad, you take the blame. There's a word for that kind of behaviour—but you're not allowed to say it on TV.

IT DOES GET BETTER | NOV. 27, 2007

Last week was National Bullying Awareness Week in Canada. Now, for those of us long out of school, it's tempting to treat that one like National Nutrition Week and ignore it altogether. But unfortunately, if you Google "bully," "Canada" and "suicide" you'll get more hits than if you were searching for "Paris Hilton" and "hotel room."

And we're not talking about one or two horror stories here—we're talking about hundreds. And the more of these stories you read, the more you realize the greatest thing about being an adult is that no matter how bad things get you never have to go to grade nine ever again. Because for a lot of kids out there going to school doesn't rank right up there as the best days of their life. Because they're different in some way, they look at going to school like some sort of prison sentence. And you can't blame them. I mean, you walk in the door when you're five years old, they keep you for twelve years, you're not allowed to leave. Cripes, in this country, you do less time for murder.

Now of course, the minute you leave school you immediately forget how bad it can be for some people. But you want to say to these kids who are being bullied, You know what? You're right. These are not the best days of your life. In fact, these are probably the worst. But after this, they get better, and then—believe it or not—they get great. Trust me: I'm one of the smartest guys I know.

And if you're being hassled because you're a geek—in a few years, you will inherit the earth. The biggest geek I went to school with was seventy-six pounds; he got hassled every day. The poor guy, he couldn't walk up a flight of steps without falling over to the left or getting a nosebleed. I have no idea how he got through it—in hindsight, he is the bravest man I know—but these days he's as happy as Larry. He runs a video game company in California. If I had his money, I'd burn mine.

And if you're being harassed in school because you're gay, the fact is, in a few years you will have more friends than you know what to do with. You can be as open as you want. Not only will you be the funniest guy in the room, but when you fly standby on Air Canada you'll get a free upgrade to business class. Because the guy behind the counter, he's gay too.

So if you're being bullied in school because you're different, please, tell someone about it, and remember, even in a real prison, eventually, everyone gets parole.

TALKING TOUGH WITH JEAN CHRÉTIEN

Ottawa.

Broadcast Nov. 20, 2007

MERCER: When people think of Jean Chrétien being prime minister we immediately think of images like the Shawinigan shake—you grabbing the guy.

CHRÉTIEN: I grabbed him by the neck.

MERCER: You did.

CHRÉTIEN: But you know, he was a bit too close—

MERCER: Am I too close now?

CHRÉTIEN: —and dangerous. It was a protester, and he came rushing to me. And I flip him over. And he lost his bridge.

MERCER: The bridge in his mouth.

CHRÉTIEN: Yes. And he asked for me to pay back that. And Donolo said to me, don't worry, Prime Minister, we'll put it on the infrastructure program.

HAVE YOU SEEN THIS MAN?

MAR. 18, 2008

People who cover politics in Canada know very well who Ezra Levant is. The rest of the country couldn't pick him out in a lineup. Which I always believed was a good thing because, without a doubt, he is one of the most aggravating men on this earth. And I only say that because—in full disclosure—he happens to be a friend of mine. I've known him for over ten years.

The last time I saw Ezra I was doing a show in Alberta. The audience, they were all conservationists. They were saving rivers. Ezra picked me up after the show for a beer. I walked out front, and there was Ezra, leaning against his Hummer smoking a cigar and, yes, the engine was running.

Which I'm sure he did purely for my benefit. The man is a provocateur, he is an agitator and now, thanks to the Alberta Human Rights Tribunal, he's become a freedom fighter. He's been defending his actions in front of that tribunal for the past two years. He has no idea when it's going to end, he has no right to a speedy trial and he has to pay his own legal costs while his accusers do not.

So what is it that Ezra did? Well, he published the *Western Standard*—in my opinion, a completely nutty magazine. He once published a column by a stay-at-home mother of nine who offered witty tips from her pastor on how to avoid your children turning out gay. But to be fair to Ezra, every time I complained he'd say the same thing: "You should write your own column. I'll publish it next week. Word for word." If nothing else, Ezra believes in freedom of speech.

Which is why I knew, when half the world exploded because some newspaper in Denmark published cartoons of the prophet Mohammed, Ezra would republish those cartoons so we could see what all the fuss was about. Yes, it would offend people, but I knew he'd do it anyway. Because that's what Ezra does. Hey, it's a free country.

Well, it used to be. Since then, he's spent over $100,000 defending his right to republish the cartoons. And his magazine—well, it went out of business. The gods of the free market took care of that. It turns out that not many people were interested in what the magazine had to say. So it's gone. But if we're not careful, if we force the Ezras in this country to shut up, our freedom of speech could be next.

TREATING US LIKE IDIOTS

H.L. Mencken said, "Nobody ever went broke underestimating the taste and intelligence of the American people." Plenty of people in Canadian politics seem to feel the same way about us.

Thankfully, in politics, once the people get the whiff that they are being taken for granted or treated like sheep, they bounce the offenders from office. In Canada, after all, we don't elect people to office so much as throw them out. Treating the electorate like idiots is the fastest way to the unemployment line.

A BOLD PLAN | MAR. 15, 2004

It has been a very busy week for Paul Martin. The revitalization of the Liberal party continues. First up, the execution of Sheila Copps was a tremendous success. The Martinites punted Sheila so hard in the head, her grandchildren are going to feel it. And let's face it, she deserved it.

Let us not forget, this is a woman who committed the ultimate sin: this is a woman who ran for the leadership of the Liberal Party of Canada. And you can't do that and get away with it. Not in that party. All the white guys in the party who wanted that job had realized this and dropped out of the race long before their names showed up on any ballot. But not Sheila. Nope, she wanted to stay in the race. And therefore they have destroyed her. Plus, let's face it, she probably bugged the hell out of them for the last decade.

That is the way things are in the Liberal Party of Canada—a party that has, wait for it, just unveiled a new logo. Can you stand the excitement? This is clearly a party revitalized. Thanks to Paul Martin, they got rid of Sheila and they got a new font, all in one week.

And now it looks as though they're going to head to the polls sooner rather than later. The idea is, once Canadians get a look at this shiny new logo and Paul Martin's smiling face, we will become so baffled that all Liberal sins will be forgiven. This is a bold plan. They've taken a clunker, they've slapped on some new paint, they're calling it brand new, and it just might work. As long as nobody looks under the hood.

But it makes me think that the Martinites are forgetting something about Canadian voters that Jean Chrétien always understood: that when it comes to politics, we're not as stunned as we look.

I'M SO SCARED | JAN. 17, 2006

There's a week to go until the big vote, and what have we learned? First of all, that negative ads work.

The Conservative ad where they've taken the ugly picture of Paul Martin and turned him red so he looks like Satan is very effective. By and large, Canadians do not like the idea of being governed by Satan, no matter how well the economy is doing. And then there are the Liberal ads. These have shown us that while negative ads work, stupid ads don't. Because the Liberals have taken stupid to a whole new level. It's an art now. It's like the Liberals woke up one morning and said, "You know, Canadians, they think we're arrogant and corrupt. Let's add stunned to the list and make it a hat trick."

I'm talking about the ads that accuse Stephen Harper of wanting to put soldiers with guns in Canadian cities. Which is true. Harper has promised to station four hundred soldiers in Vancouver, Calgary, Regina and Winnipeg, to deal with natural disasters. And the Liberals made it sound as though Harper had some freaky plan to enact martial law. Because Canadians are afraid of soldiers, right? Wrong.

I can guarantee you, whoever created that ad has never met anyone in the Canadian Forces, has never been around anyone in the Canadian Forces. I have—hundreds of them, all of them carrying guns—and I never felt so safe in my life. Cripes, there's twenty-four thousand soldiers in Atlantic Canada alone. The last time I bumped into three soldiers, in the middle of the night, in Halifax, do you know what they did to me? They pushed my car out of a snowbank.

Now personally, I don't know why we need four hundred soldiers standing around at all times in downtown Regina waiting for a natural disaster. Maybe Stephen Harper's aware of some sort of natural-disaster prophecy that I'm not aware of. I do know this, though. If you treat Canadians like idiots, you will lose. That's not a prophecy, that's a fact. A fact the Liberals are about to find out.

FIVE AND COUNTING | APR. 18, 2006

In politics, some people—cynical people, not people like me—believe the name of the game is fooling people. To them, success is treating the electorate like a bunch of dummies and then getting away with it. Well, if that's the case, I'm starting to think Stephen Harper is some kind of genius.

The perfect example is this five priorities stuff. That is the new mantra in Conservative Ottawa. This government has five priorities and only five. And for a long time I thought this was a good idea. I thought, this Harper, he's a very focused man. But then the more I thought about it, I came to realize that a government with just five priorities is completely idiotic. I mean, imagine if you had to do that in your own life—pick your priorities and stop at five. Most Canadians would say, okay, well I guess I have to feed and clothe the kids and give them shelter and send them to school and keep them healthy. Bang, that's it! Five! You can accomplish nothing else. Congratulations, you're now a very successful Amish person.

Most Canadians can't live their life like that, so I don't know where Harper gets off thinking that's the way to run a country. Five priorities doesn't cut it when you factor in ten provinces, three territories, thirty-five million people, a war in Afghanistan and a record number of smog days. When I was growing up my mother could do fourteen things at once with her eyes closed, and she had a full-time job. I want a prime minister who can accomplish at least half that. So aim high, Stephen.

Whatever you think, Canadian voters can count higher than five.

THE RIGHT WOMAN | NOV. 20, 2006

I have never endorsed a political candidate before, but now the time has come.

Like most Canadians, I am watching the campaign leading up to the by-election in London, Ontario, with bated breath. It's a barnburner of a race, and there's no doubt that all of the parties have fielded strong candidates. It's my belief, however, that one candidate stands head and shoulders above the rest. If I could vote in this one, I would have to mark an X for Dianne Haskett.

I also believe it is a testament to the Conservative party that it can attract a candidate of Ms. Haskett's stature. My goodness, they had to look all the way to Washington, DC, to find her.

The fact that Ms. Haskett has been in America working for the Republican party for the past six years may seem like a deficit at first glance, but I say every cloud has a silver lining. It will be easy to spot the Tory candidate in the Santa Claus Parade this Saturday: just look for the car with the American licence plates and the Bush-Cheney sticker.

Predictably, some local Tories are upset that Ottawa hand-picked the candidate it wanted over the wishes of the local riding association, but let's face it, that's just sour grapes. Having a puppet of the Prime Minister's Office is an honour for the people of London.

In fact the Prime Minister's Office has so much confidence in Ms. Haskett's ability, it actually owns her. Well, it doesn't own her, of course, but it does own her name. These days the single most important tool of any politician is his or her Internet identity. In Dianne's case, she doesn't control her online identity—the Conservative Party of Canada does. In fact the party bought her domain name days before she was given the nomination. The party also owns her office furniture, photocopier and portable sound system.

From the prime minister's perspective, owning a candidate's name is simply an effective and proven way of controlling people.

In the sixties, radio stations in the United States used to make a practice of owning the on-air names of "Negro DJs." That way, if disc jockeys ever stepped out of line, the station could not only fire them but stop them from working under those names for anyone else. Of course, this name-owning practice has long been abandoned, because apparently it's despicable. Nice to see it resurrected in the Prime Minister's Office. My guess is that some keen whipper-snapper in the head office was reading up on the civil rights movement in the United States and got some good ideas while they were at it.

London is crawling with these Ottawa-based political operatives these days. PMO staffers and minister's aides have been bussed into the riding on a regular basis, each armed with a Mapquest printout and a list highlighting the names of local malls. They go door to door for Dianne making sure to drop local references into the conversation so they can dupe the person on the step into believing they grew up six streets over. Look out, London—this is the big time.

This on-the-ground support from Team Calgary is an encouraging sign from head office. They know that with Dianne Haskett, they have a winner on their hands.

In politics, being ahead of the curve is the sign of true greatness. Some candidates can talk a good game, but Dianne has a solid record.

For example, she was against gay rights long before that became trendy. When the rest of the country was blasé about the homosexual threat, Dianne was alerting all who would listen that the homos were on the march. When she did a stint as mayor of London in the nineties, she consistently went out of her way to stop the gays. At the time she made it clear that "appearing to endorse homosexuality is turning my back on God and the day I turn my back on God I lose my authority as Mayor." Give this woman a seat in the House of Commons!

Did she get the credit she deserved way back when? No. Instead, the city she ran was fined $10,000 by the Ontario Human Rights Commission for violating the rights of gay taxpayers. In response, Dianne locked herself in her own house for three weeks in an act of self-imposed house arrest. Frankly, Dianne could give lessons on how to be a drama queen.

History now shows us that it is Dianne who got the last laugh. Here it is, 2006, and Canada is on the brink of destruction because some car salesman named Larry intends to marry a pipefitter named Frank in Flin Flon.

Of course that could change the minute the Tories get a majority, which is why so many senior ministers are thrilled that Dianne is on the ballot. The man with the purse, President of the Treasury Board John Baird, travelled to London to endorse Haskett and went as far as to call her the "accountability candidate."

This is a coup for the Haskett campaign. John Baird's credentials as a Conservative are unblemished except for his unfortunate mistake of saying that he would vote in favour of same-sex marriage if it ever came up. By going out of his way to get Haskett elected, Baird is effectively negating his own vote on the issue. I hope John Baird receives some sort of award from the Conservative party for this selfless act. Perhaps they could arrange a nice sit-down dinner where they give Baird a break from his usual duties and hire a dancing monkey instead.

I don't mean to imply that Dianne is a single-issue candidate. She not only has great insight on what adults should be allowed to do in the privacy of their bedrooms, she also has views on who one should worship and who one should fear. In 1996 she took part in a public prayer breakfast where people were encouraged to bow their heads and pray that Canada be protected "from the darkness and deception of the spirit of Islam."

This is a very impressive record. Let's remember that

encouraging Canadians to be afraid of other religions wasn't even on the radar in 1996. In fact, Canadians have never been big on the idea of domestic holy wars, and yet there was Dianne, back in the day, trying to stir it up old school.

Some people are uniters and some people are dividers; Dianne is a uniter. In fact, "Uniting majorities against minorities since 1996" was under consideration as a potential campaign slogan.

I can only pray that if Stephen Harper ever needs a parliamentary secretary in charge of breeding religious intolerance, Dianne will be there in the House ready to heed the call.

And finally, above all else, I think Dianne should be commended for her commitment to silence. She has remained largely hidden during the campaign, refusing all national media requests and most local media requests. With her reluctance to speak about the issues, she has shown the people of London that they have in Dianne Haskett a candidate who is willing to sit down, shut up and do what she is told.

If the residents of London feel that best describes them, electing her will certainly prove it.

LIBERAL TERROR | FEB. 28, 2007

Parliamentary Secretary to the President of the Treasury Board and Conservative MP Pierre Poilievre appeared on radio in Ottawa recently with explosive information. In a discussion about terrorism, he revealed that the Conservatives now know that the Liberal party is a haven for extremist groups and that Liberal leader Stéphane Dion has collapsed under their power, a puppet for said extremist elements, whom one assumes are pro-terror.

When asked directly if Liberal MP Navdeep Bains was an extremist, Pierre took the high road and refused to answer; clearly he knows something we don't.

"I don't comment on individuals," he said. "But what I would say is we know there is an extremist element in the Liberal party, generally, that has been very vocal in opposing measures that are designed to combat terrorism. And it would seem that Mr. Dion has collapsed under the pressure from those groups."

I for one cannot believe that tanks are not rolling in the streets.

I think based on Pierre's comments we should be afraid. We should be very afraid. If a major political party in Canada has been hijacked by terrorists, then we have to get to the bottom of it. And make no mistake, Pierre is not a loose cannon on HMCS *Harper.* He is a trusted and devoted crew member.

There *are* no more Tory loose cannons. The days of the grassroots are long dead. Conservative cabinet ministers are not allowed to do any media in this country without the express permission of Sandra Buckler, the prime minister's director of communications. Freedom of speech extends to Conservative MPs when Sandra says it does. If Sandra says, "Stand on your two hind legs and dance," the finance minister barks, "Irish jig or the hully gully?"

You can be sure that Pierre's confirmation of a terrorist insurrection within the Liberal party came directly from Madame Buckler.

I suggest a full round of televised hearings chaired by none other than Monsieur Poilievre. Every card-carrying Liberal should be paraded in front of the cameras and made to answer his questions.

Are they now or have they ever been a member of any group? Do they know Navdeep Bains? Have they ever socialized with him or someone who looks like him? These are questions that should be answered.

Pierre is the right man for the job. If you go to his website and read his biography you will see he is an accomplished young man who worked as an office intern at Magna and also wrote an essay once.

And as far as extremist groups go, Pierre is a member of only two organizations. He is a member of the Conservative Party of Canada and the Blue Label Club. As Pierre explained to the press after his re-election, the Blue Label Club is a members-only group of young male Conservative MPs who gather to drink Johnny Walker Blue Label scotch. The price may be extreme, but not the members.

I hope all Canadians join me in wishing Pierre best of luck in eradicating extremism and exposing the Liberal party as a haven for terror.

Go, Pierre, go!

ANGRY JIM | OCT. 30, 2007

Minister of Finance Jim Flaherty is a man with his finger on the pulse.

In politics, if you can figure out what's making Canadians angry you're halfway to the finish line. But that's where Jim pulls a face plant.

Take tax cuts, for example. Jim knows Canadians want a personal income tax cut. And my God, if it was up to Jim, he would give us one. He believes it so much he trembles when he says it, and shakes his little hands at the heavens. The only problem is, it *is* up to Jim, and he's been in charge for almost two years now, he's up to his neck in surpluses, and *still* we haven't seen a tax cut.

Then there are bank fees. Jim knows the banks are screwing the little guy, so what's Jim do?

He gets so angry his head almost comes off, and he's on the front page of every newspaper in the country telling us that the big bad bankers are on notice. Exactly what are these bankers on notice for, Jim? A golf game? Or a fundraiser? Because they certainly didn't lower their bank fees.

So no surprise that Jim now wants us to know that yes, we are paying more for goods in Canada than in the United States. And what's he going to do about it? Surprise, surprise, it's the angry leprechaun act again.

This is the Conservative party's approach to helping out the little guy. Hire a satellite truck to pull up to a Tim

Horton's, get yourself on the news drinking a double-double and tell Canadians you feel their pain. And we are supposed to go, "Hey, honey, look—Jim goes to Tim Horton's, we go to Tim Horton's. We're angry and he's angry. He must be standing up for Canada."

No, actually, he's treating us like we're idiots.

They say the definition of insanity is doing the same thing over and over again and hoping for a different result. So either Jim's nuts for thinking we're going to keep buying this act, or we are for believing a word he says.

SCIENCE FRICTION

You don't need a Nobel Prize to work out that a nuclear power plant ought to have a safety backup system, that climate change is a problem worth discussing, and that—meteorologically speaking—it's likely to get cold in Canada in the winter.

TORONTARDED | DEC. 4, 2007

Canadians love to talk about the weather—always have, and always will. It's what we do. We have always been passionate about the weather, but we have never been hysterical about the weather, and certainly we have never been afraid of the weather. But suddenly, that seems to be changing.

At first, I thought this was a Toronto thing. Because when you move to Toronto you realize pretty quick that when it comes to the weather there are two parallel universes. There's what you hear about in the media, and then there's what you see out your window. You can wake up and turn on the news and see a lead story about a snowstorm that slammed the city, how there were three hundred accidents between 5 and 9 in the morning, how no flights took off. And the reporter on the scene is so panicked he sounds like he's reporting live from the bottom of a collapsed mine shaft. And you think, "Oh my God, I had no idea, those poor people."

But then you realize: hang on, I'm in Toronto. And you look out the window and see there's three centimetres of snow on the ground and the kid on the street walking a dog is wearing a T-shirt.

There was no snowstorm. There was no weather bomb. There were flurries. And then it got windy and the entire city ground to a halt.

It's why I invented the word "Torontarded." Comes in handy, believe me. But before the rest of the country gets all cocky, know this: weather hysteria is spreading across this nation like some sort of demented low-pressure system.

We don't have forecasts anymore, we have weathertainment. It's designed to scare the hell out of you. Cold weather and snow are now reported as though it was raining frogs or there was a plague of locusts out there. Problem is, cold weather is not a sign of a coming apocalypse. It's just business as usual in Canada. But tell that to the crowd at the Weather Network. If you listened to them for five minutes, you wouldn't leave the house for five months.

This is the true north strong and free, and cold, and wet, and icy, and dark—sometimes all at once. It's why God invented long johns. This is Canada. We have winter. Embrace it.

COME ON IN, THE WATER'S FINE | JAN. 15, 2008

Like most Canadians, I'm pretty ignorant when it comes to nuclear power plants. I mean, I know we have them. They seem to work. Other than that, it's all good. And for some reason I walk around having faith that the government, or someone, has a system in place to ensure that they're safe and they're up to date. After all, this is a country where you can't buy a hockey helmet unless it's got a CSA-approved sticker slapped on the sucker.

So I didn't like waking up in the morning and reading that a nuclear power plant in Chalk River that was built in 1957, when Diefenbaker was prime minister, had been closed because the people in charge hadn't bothered to install their legally required safety backup system. That's not a good story. That's a bad story. That's a heads-should-roll kind of story.

Now, normally in these situations the buck should stop with the minister in charge. That would be Gary Lunn, Minister of Natural Resources, who, as it turns out, knew four months ago that this plant didn't have a safety backup system and did absolutely nothing. That's not a problem according to Gary, because in his opinion the plant doesn't need one. And Gary should know. After all, this is a man who spent most of his professional life teaching public education courses on home renovation contracts. So, by all means, if you want to know if you should run your rain pipe down the left or right side of your house, call Gary. But other than that, everything this man knows about nuclear power he basically learned from reading a Spider-Man comic.

And then we have our prime minister, Stephen Harper. He blames the whole thing on the Liberals. And not because a Liberal didn't install the backup system, but because the woman who blew the whistle on the power plant was appointed by the Liberals. She's also an expert on nuclear power and the head of the Canadian Nuclear Safety Commission. And Stephen Harper, an economist by trade, now wants her fired.

Harper is like the mayor in *Jaws* saying, "We can't close the beach, it's the long weekend, the tourists are coming." Except in this movie, the woman who stood up for Canada, the one who blew the whistle, is the one who might get eaten.

SCARED STUPID BY SCIENCE | FEB. 19, 2008

When twenty-year-old Ellen Page from Halifax got an Academy Award nomination for best actress, we all cheered. When our hockey team won gold at the World Juniors, we all cheered. You don't have to be a movie fan or a hockey fan to be moved by this stuff. You just have to be a Canadian.

And likewise, you don't have to be a genius to be very proud of the fact that Canadian scientists won the Nobel Peace Prize. I mean, this is the mother of all prizes. In fact, they gave one to Mother Teresa.

So what happened this past week when those winning Canadian scientists came to Parliament Hill for a reception in their honour with their Nobel Prize tucked beneath their arms? Prime Minister Harper, the guy whose job it is to represent us at these things, refused to attend. The Canadian cabinet refused to attend. And why? Because these scientists, who—I don't know if I've mentioned this or not—won the Nobel Peace Prize, had the gall to do it by formulating a plan to fight climate change. And my guess is it doesn't call for an increase in oil sands production. So as a result, not a single cabinet minister would cross the hall and shake the scientists' hands.

Now remember, this is the same government that just recently fired the national science adviser—a guy whose job it was to advise the prime minister and cabinet on all issues pertaining to science. They just didn't see the need for that guy. With this crowd, being a science adviser is a bit like being the Maytag repairman. The phone just doesn't ring.

What I want to know is: how did we get here? Canadian scientists gave humankind the polio vaccine. We discovered insulin. Heck—we even invented the Robertson screwdriver. And suddenly science is the new enemy.

I understand that in politics people and parties have enemies, and destroying your enemy is the name of the game. That's the way you win. But we cannot allow the government to declare war on knowledge, otherwise we all lose.

Unless of course they start passing out Nobel Prizes for idiocy.

FREEZING WITH DAVID SUZUKI

DS and RM prepare to jump into a very cold lake. Gravenhurst, Ontario. Broadcast Feb. 13, 2007

SUZUKI: I'm too old for this. I'm not going to do it.

MERCER: You're going to do it.

SUZUKI: I'm not going to do it. You're not even paying me, for God's sake.

MERCER: You're doing it for the planet.

SUZUKI: I'm going to freeze my nuts off, you know.

MERCER: For the planet—

SUZUKI: The planet? Hell—what about my nuts?

SPENDING LIKE CRAZY

I have a friend who came out of the womb as a rabid fiscal conservative. It has been a wonder to watch him over the last decade work tirelessly against the odds to defeat the big-spending Liberals. It has been equally wonderful watching his reaction to a Conservative government that has yet to deliver a single personal income tax cut. It's like watching a man at forty come to the realization that there is no Easter Bunny. There is, however, a Santa, his name is Stephen Harper and he has gifts for everyone with the exception of the fiscal conservatives who got him elected in the first place.

WHY CHINA? | JAN. 24, 2005

There's no doubt about it, Canadians support the idea of foreign aid. It's part of our job as a first-world nation. But at the risk of sounding like a moron, what the hell are we sending money to China for? China has one of the largest economies on earth, and we're sending them $60 million a year in foreign aid. This is a country that might as well own the trademark on the phrase "emerging superpower." A phrase, by the way, which will never, ever be used to describe Canada.

Maybe I'm wrong, but I always thought the point of foreign aid was for us to give money to countries that didn't have any money. China? China spent $20 billion on their Olympic bid. Not that you can blame them. If you want to convince the world that Tiananmen Square is the best place on earth to hold beach volleyball, you're going to need to spend the big bucks. Never mind the fact they have a huge army with actual helicopters that can take off and land. Or that they have a space program with a planned mission to Mars.

Wouldn't our $60 million in aid be better off going to Sudan—which, you know, doesn't have a space program? Because as it stands now, I don't know what the Chinese word for "sucker" is, but I bet when Canada comes up in conversation there, that word gets used a lot.

BACK TO SCHOOL DAYS | JAN. 10, 2006

Usually when there's an election, there's a script that both sides follow, and the rest of us read along. We all know our parts. In a federal election, the leaders fly around the country and make all sorts of promises that we take with a grain of salt. But based on those promises, we decide who we're going to vote for.

But the promises, whether they're kept or not, are generally within the realm of sanity. This time is completely different. The leaders are acting like this isn't a real federal election, or a provincial election, or even a municipal election for that matter. And for the longest time, I couldn't figure out what it was that it reminded me of. And then it dawned on me: high school student council.

In high school elections, 90 per cent of the candidates are very serious, but some guy always gets up there, high as a kite, and makes all sorts of insane announcements, and everyone loves him. When I was in grade ten, some dude with a mullet promised free beer in the fountains and a smoking room inside the school. My, how we cheered. And that's what Martin and Harper are like. Or they're like divorced parents trying to buy their children's love. We're the kids, they're our two dads. Except this time they're not trying to buy our love with just an Xbox or a few Easy-Bake Ovens.

No, they've gone completely off their heads. Martin is spending like Belinda Stronach in a shoe store. We're talking billions of dollars every time he turns around. And Harper is outspending him. There's a rumour going around that Harper's about to promise everyone in Ontario a Ferris wheel and a pony.

This is not good, Canada. I hate to be old-fashioned here, but Stephen, Paul—where in God's name is all the money coming from? It's a bad sign when the worst-case scenario is that whoever wins this election actually keeps his promises. Because at the end of the day, free beer in the fountain is a great idea—I just don't want to pay for it.

GIVE THEM TIME | MAR. 27, 2007

When the first Conservative budget came out over a year ago, Tories everywhere said the same thing: that it didn't really look like a Conservative budget, but give them time. Wait until next year, they said, then you'll see a Conservative government in action.

And you can't blame the Tories for being a little antsy. They just came off twelve years of Liberal rule. They were down to their last nerve. It seems to me that for most of my natural life you could not have a conversation with a Tory that didn't end up with them this close to having a stroke because they were so angry at the Liberals for not giving them a personal tax cut and for spending too much money in Quebec.

Well, thank God those days are over, eh? Now we have a Conservative government in Ottawa, they're in control of the agenda, they're ahead in the polls and they just released their second budget. And what happened? They're spending like drunken Liberals. Stephen Harper is like Paul Martin on three bottles of rye.

Jim Flaherty is now officially the biggest-spending finance minister in Canadian history—and that's saying something. And the amazing thing is, he managed to spend all that money and not give a single Canadian a cut in personal income tax. Instead, he decided to send an extra three billion dollars—*three thousand million dollars*— to Quebec.

And what's Quebec going to do with that money? They're going to give the people a personal income tax cut. That noise you can hear is the sound of blood vessels bursting in the heads of Tory voters across the country.

The taps are back on in Ottawa. Tory times are good times. It's like the good old days of Brian Mulroney—minus the deficits. But let's face it, at this rate it's just a matter of time.

THE UNDEKE-ABLE WOMAN

Broadcast Jan. 31, 2005

MARGARET ATWOOD: As the late Robertson Davies once told me, "Peggy, a good goalie anticipates play. A *great* goalie influences play." That's why I like to come out aggressively to cut down the angle. If the shooter can't see net, he'll deke. And you don't deke Margaret.

SCANDALOUS BEHAVIOUR

I remember when the scandal story broke. The auditor general's report showed hundreds of millions of dollars had been wasted and we had to recall our ambassador from Denmark. This is outrageous, I thought—we have an ambassador in Denmark? And what a huge sum of money was involved! Two hundred and fifty million dollars. Imagine what you could do with that. Give it to the National Film Board, and you could have yourself a seven-minute cartoon.

MEMORY MAN | FEB. 16, 2004

I've seen a few auditor general's reports in my time, but this one takes the cake. Not that the report itself was shocking—no, these things happen all the time. It's like Groundhog Day. Every year around this time, the auditor general sticks her head out of her hole and tells us that the Liberals are wasting all our money. What I found shocking was Prime Minister Martin's revelation that yet again he had no idea what was going on.

I'm not a medical doctor, but I'm starting to get a"Pappy's getting older" vibe off Paul Martin. According to him, he has absolutely no knowledge of anything that this government's been doing for the past ten years. Plus he has no knowledge of anything his own company's been doing for the last ten years. It's like he woke up in a bed with a doctor standing over him saying, "Mr. Martin, Mr. Martin, it's 2004. For the past ten years you've owned an international shipping empire and you've been Canada's minister of finance." And Martin's like, "No, no. That's impossible. The last thing I remember is Rita MacNeil finally got her own variety show."

It's like he's got acute memory loss or early dementia. How else can you explain the fact that for the few months he's been on the job, so far all he's done is look into a camera and say, "I don't know, I had no idea, it wasn't me, I wasn't there." Throw in an evil twin and we've got the makings of one hell of a movie of the week—complete with bad acting.

FROM THE DESK OF PRIME MINISTER MARTIN | JULY 5, 2005

Dear former friend and Liberal campaign donor,

As you might have read in recent media reports, donations for the Liberal Party of Canada are at an all-time low. The numbers below tell the tale.

Total personal donations for 2004:

- Conservatives: $10.9 million
- Liberals: $5.2 million
- New Democrats: $5.19 million
- Bloc Québécois: $897,000

Our records indicate that you were once an active supporter of the Liberal party but no longer send cheques or answer the phone when we call. Your request for a lawn sign in the event of the coming election seems to have been lost in the mail.

As you are no doubt aware, a cabinet minister was in your area recently and dropped by your residence to speak with you directly about this situation. Unfortunately you were otherwise engaged at the time, choosing instead to lie on the floor with your family with the lights off. I understand the importance of family time and suggest you call us and tell us when an appropriate time for such a visit would be.

Many of you have voiced concern about corruption inside the Liberal party, and have specifically mentioned being turned off by the notion of so-called envelopes of cash being passed around sleazy Montreal diners.

As your leader, I understand that if mysterious envelopes of cash are being passed around, you—the rank and file, the former supporters, the backbone of the party—would feel angry and left out at not receiving one.

That said, let me tell you about our new donor program: the Laurier Club Clearinghouse Sweepstakes!

From now on, when you donate $1,000 to the Liberal party, you too will receive a fat envelope that may or may not contain one or more of the following.

- Membership of the Laurier Club
- Valuable Mark's Work Warehouse coupons
- Ten thousand dollars in unmarked twenties and fifties

This time everyone gets an envelope!

I hope that you will consider this carefully.

Thank you for your consideration.

Sincerely,
Paul Martin, Leader
Liberal Party of Canada
P.S. Please pick up your phone.

WITH EXTRA CHEESE | FEB. 7, 2005

Any time a cabinet minister resigns because of a scandal, that's a huge body blow for any government. For a minority government, it could be devastating. That's why the rule is, if you're the prime minister, you will do everything in your power short of murder to stop any resignations.

Look at Brian Mulroney. He had a whack of resignations, and it stuck with him forever. Rightly or wrongly, when you think about Mulroney, you think scandal. So then along came Chrétien, and Chrétien said okay, well, there will be no more of that. As the saying goes, the only thing that could force a Chrétien cabinet minister to resign was being caught in bed with a dead girl or a live boy.

Paul Martin clearly has different views on this, because he's the one who accepted Judy Sgro's resignation in the first place. And why did she resign? What massive scandal forced Canada's immigration minister from office? Some guy said that he gave her free pizza in exchange for political favours. It can be truly embarrassing what can pass for a scandal in this country. And the capper is, the guy making the allegations is a convicted child smuggler who's been ordered deported from Canada half a dozen times.

We've become so cynical about politics that we're eager to believe the word of a career criminal over a cabinet minister. That says a lot about the state of politics in Canada. None of it very good. But at the same time, looking back over the last decade, I can't help but think, I wish I knew back then what I've learned now. Because if I'd known a few pizzas could take down a cabinet minister, I would've had Pizza Pizza on speed-dial long ago.

JUST LIKE OLD TIMES | FEB. 28, 2006

There's been a lot said about the office of the prime minister over the years, but I've never heard it said that the actual office may, in fact, cause lunacy.

But just look, for a second, at Prime Minister Martin. It's as if the day that he took office, he completely lost his compass.

I'm not saying he didn't know the difference between right and wrong. I'm suggesting he lost it. I don't know if the poor man knows the difference between up and down. And then to make matters worse, it's like someone gave him a pair of scissors and told him to spend eighteen months running up and down the stairs of the Parliament buildings. He just knew this was going to end badly.

Now to be fair, I thought this was a Paul Martin phenomenon. I thought that he wanted that job so badly that when he finally got it, something melted in his frontal lobe. But along comes Stephen Harper, and I'm starting to see similarities.

I have a confession to make. During the election campaign, I got a little caught up in this whole "Stand up for Canada" thing Harper was preaching. I'd watch him give one of his stump speeches on accountability, ethics and Senate reform, and I'd think, "You know, I don't have to agree with everything this man stands for, but wouldn't it be nice if, for once, we had a prime minister who did everything on the up and up?" I was starting to have, for lack of a better word, faith.

So in many ways, it's a stinking relief to see that a Harper government can be every bit as sleazy as any that came before him. Who could have imagined after all that blather about Senate reform that on the day Stephen Harper became prime minister he would appoint a buddy of his from Quebec to the Senate and then put him right into the cabinet?

This man has never been elected to anything, and now he's a cabinet minister. Talk about being entitled to your entitlements. I never noticed that in the Tory Blue Book. And I must have skipped the part altogether where they were going to use cabinet seats to bribe people to cross the floor.

The Liberals have done all this before, and now the Tories are doing it too. And so, in record time, Stephen

Harper has gone from being a man promising to stand up for Canada to being a politician who says the end justifies the means. Which may prove to be confusing, because until recently, the Liberals owned that slogan.

FROM THE DESK OF MACKENZIE KING | SEPT. 25, 2006

Dear friend and supporter,

Did you know that in the event of your tragic death you can remain an active member of the Liberal Party of Canada? The party's Membership Renewal Commission has reinterpreted our constitution and has determined that dead people can now hold executive positions within the Liberal party and even attend future conventions as voting members.

This is why I am writing to you today.

Please consider a one-time gift of your human remains to the party—at no cost to you.

Imagine the peace of mind you will have on your deathbed knowing that while death may bring an end to many of life's pleasures, you will still be involved in the advancement of democracy and Liberal ideals in Canada.

Many Canadians are doing just that right now. Michael Ignatieff has a number of deceased Canadians working for him on his campaign. They may be dead, but they can still get Iggy with it! In fact World War I flying ace Billy Bishop has recently taken out a party membership and has officially endorsed Ignatieff and the courageous positions he has taken on the use of force during the interrogation of prisoners.

But while Billy Bishop's arrival back on the scene is certain to bring some excitement to this campaign, it is Joe Volpe who should be commended for pioneering this exciting new way to support the Liberal party. As Joe has said so eloquently in the past, for the Liberal party to succeed in the twenty-first century, we must embrace not only hard-working new Canadians, but non-working dead Canadians as well.

It was Joe who realized early on that the dead were a huge untapped resource, signing up as many of these dedicated dead Liberals as he could. In fact, after a hard day of campaigning in the many small towns across Canada, Joe would often, under cover of darkness, visit local graveyards. Once there, Joe, armed with artist parchment and a number four charcoal pencil, would make tombstone rubbings until dawn—every rubbing a testament to a life lived, and the basis for a party membership.

So if you are dead or near dead, hurry now and give your body to the party—all the leadership candidates are looking for support from dead people.

Bob Rae, for example, has recently accepted the public endorsement of Hedy Fry.

So we ask you now in the event of your death—remember the Liberal Party of Canada. Also, in the event of your near death, say, a car accident or heart attack, take the opportunity to ask your deceased relatives if they would like to support the party.

Donate your body today by downloading a donor declaration of intent from the Liberal party website.

Do it for Canada.

Yours truly,
Mackenzie King, Chair
Membership Renewal Commission
Liberal Party of Canada

FREDO MULRONEY | NOV. 20, 2007

Brian Mulroney has always been one of the most polarizing characters in Canadian history. That's his shtick. You mention his name anywhere in Canada, half the room wants to snap. And now, like some sort of dormant gastrointestinal virus, he's back demanding and getting a full judicial inquiry into his dealings with Karlheinz Schreiber. And you can't blame the man, really—last time they looked into this he walked away with over two million dollars.

What I find amazing about this whole affair is the government's reaction. Because, let's face it, everyone on earth knows that Brian Mulroney took $300,000 in cash from Karlheinz Schreiber. If Stephen Harper didn't know that, the man needs a CATscan. He knew, he just didn't care. Until last week, he called Mulroney a valuable adviser, a confidant, a friend. He had him over to the house for dinner, they went up to the cottage together, they spoke on the phone. So what does Prime Minister Harper do when a friend gets in trouble? He calls a press conference and announces to the world that Brian Mulroney is now dead to him. And then he orders everyone in the party who is a friend of Mulroney's to treat him like Fredo in *The Godfather*.

And they did.

Look at Marjory LeBreton. Sure, she's a cabinet minister, but she's one of Mulroney's oldest friends. She goes to his children's weddings. They talk on the phone every day. If Marjory croaked tomorrow, he'd be one of her pallbearers. But nope, there's Marjory, proud as punch in the Montreal *Gazette* saying she's going to follow orders. She's not going to speak to Mulroney again until this thing is settled.

If I had friends like that, I'd want to shoot myself. Because we've all been there when someone close to us does something wrong or is accused of doing something wrong. It happens. And you have to decide: are you going to head for the hills, or are you going do the honourable thing and call the poor shagger up and take him to lunch?

Well, there's been very little honourable behaviour displayed in Ottawa this week. But as they say, there's no honour among thieves. And no honour among Tories either.

HARPER'S CRAZY WEEK | MAR. 11, 2008

What a great week in Ottawa. And by "great" I mean filled with scandals, most of them involving Prime Minister Harper. Jack Layton was on CNN talking to Lou Dobbs for God's sakes, which does not happen every day.

But if I had to pick my favourite scandal of recent days it would have to be the Cadman affair. Did the Conservative party offer Chuck Cadman, a member of Parliament who was dying, a million-dollar life insurance policy in exchange for his vote? Because that's what his widow says. But you don't have to take her word for it—Stephen Harper is on a tape saying yes, financial considerations were offered to a dying man. Well, if you buy the adage that where there's smoke there's fire, there's so much smoke coming out of this sucker, you can see it on Google Maps.

And so what does Stephen Harper say now? Forget my voice on the tape, the only thing we offered Chuck Cadman was a chance to join the Conservative party. Stephen, no offence, but that's the stupidest thing I've ever heard in my life. Could you imagine if you were on your deathbed and a couple of Tories came over to your house to try to buy you off, and they offered you membership of the Conservative party? Because, apparently, a lot of people on their deathbed think, "I wish I spent more time with the Tories."

And so what's Harper's reaction once the opposition started asking questions? He's suing. He's suing the leader of the opposition. Never before in the history of Canadian democracy has a prime minister sued the leader of the opposition. But that's what Harper's doing. Suddenly he's like that guy on TV from upstate New York who will sue anyone anytime for anything. His coffee's too hot—he will sue. Ask him a question outside of Question Period—he will sue. With a lawsuit, by the way, that is going to cost taxpayers millions and millions of dollars. Our money—being spent to ensure the prime minister won't answer any questions that should be answered.

Yes, it's been a crazy week, and it could also be a tipping point. Because Stephen Harper has always had one ace in the hole: his reputation as a straight shooter. Well, you can wave that goodbye; because when it comes to preserving reputations, Conrad Black had a better week.

VISITING PAUL MARTIN

24 Sussex Drive.
Broadcast Oct. 25, 2004

MERCER: Have you ever had to get a world leader on the phone like that [*Snaps fingers*]?

MARTIN: Yeah.

MERCER: You can get Tony Blair on the phone?

MARTIN: Yeah. Probably. Yeah.

MERCER: That's pretty cool.

MARTIN: You want to talk to him?

MERCER: *Yes.*

MARTIN: I could call him and say, "Listen, Tony, there's this guy who won't leave until he talks to you . . ."

LEST WE FORGET

BANNING PRIVATE RYAN | NOV. 22, 2004

I've always believed that in the United States there's a big difference between conservative and stupid. But boy, it's getting harder by the minute to prove that one.

On Veteran's Day in America, the movie *Saving Private Ryan* was dumped by over sixty ABC affiliates. And why? Well apparently, it's against family values. And so a whole bunch of family values groups, they got together. And they decided that because they didn't want to watch this movie, nobody should be allowed to watch this movie.

So they lobbied the FCC and they threatened to boycott any channel that would dare air this film. And it worked. The movie was removed from schedules in one-third of the country. Why? Because these people believe it is immoral to celebrate Veterans Day by watching a war movie if, get this, it contains violence, swearing or taking the Lord's name in vain. None of which of course happened in World War II. No. Because in World War II, people were too busy getting killed trying to protect America from the type of person who would definitely tell you what you can and cannot watch.

According to these people, everyone would be much better off celebrating Veterans Day by just staying at home and watching another episode of *Touched by an Angel*. Thanks to family values, when it comes to freedom and personal choice, the wheels are off the bus in America. And let's face it, it was a pretty short bus to begin within.

MEMORIAL DAY IN NEWFOUNDLAND | JULY 1, 2005

Thanks to one of those great Newfoundland-in-Confederation ironies, Canada Day is an official day of mourning in Newfoundland. You see, Canada just happens to celebrate its birthday on the anniversary of the bloodiest day in Newfoundland history.

On July 1, 1916, the Newfoundland Regiment was wiped out on the battlefield of Beaumont-Hamel, France, during the Battle of the Somme. The story of the Newfoundland Regiment in World War I is a dramatic one, long and filled with heroic victories. It came to an end on this day in 1916.

It was on this day that 801 fighting Newfoundlanders left the trenches and tried to smash through the German lines. Only 69 returned to answer the roll call. An entire generation was wiped out in minutes. Today is the day we remember them.

I was at the War Memorial in St. John's this morning at 11:00 a.m. and watched the wreath-laying ceremony. It was a beautiful day; there was a big crowd, including lots of young people, in attendance.

It makes for a bit of a muddled holiday. On the day we are supposed to be celebrating the flag, the flags are flying at half mast.

Everything is different in Newfoundland.

PRIORITY SIX | APR. 25, 2006

The Conservative government has said that it will not lower the flag on the Peace Tower as a sign of respect for the soldiers who were recently killed in Afghanistan. The government wishes to make it clear that this is not meant to disrespect soldiers who pay the ultimate price, but quite the opposite. According to the Conservative government, it's actually more respectful this way.

In defending this position, Minister of Defence Gordon O'Connor somehow blamed Jean Chrétien. From what I can gather, the Conservative position is that Chrétien was wrong to start lowering the flag in the first place, and he was often inconsistent. This is what the Conservatives do when they get their backs up. By this time tomorrow, they will be saying they want to lower the flag but can't because they are simply too outraged over the sponsorship scandal to lift their arms and pull on the ropes at the base of the pole.

It should be pointed out that when the Conservatives were in opposition, they demanded that the flag fly at half mast in similar circumstances as a sign of respect for the deceased. Now that they are in power, they have changed their minds.

In case you are wondering what the official protocol is for this type of thing, here's the relevant section from the Department of Heritage website:

> The flag on the Peace Tower of the Parliament Building at Ottawa is flown at half-mast:
>
> - on the death of a Lieutenant Governor;
> - on the death of a Canadian Privy Councillor, a Senator, or a Member of the House of Commons;
> - on the death of a person whom it is desired to honour.

This is a pretty straightforward list.

Everyone knows what lieutenant governors are: they are an elite group of politically connected senior citizens who represent the Queen in each of the provinces. These brave men and women are required to attend cocktail receptions on a daily basis for their country. When their livers explode, the flag is lowered as a sign of respect.

The fact that the flag is lowered "on the death of a Canadian Privy Councillor" will come as a surprise to the many Canadians who aren't sure what a Canadian privy councillor is. The Canadian Privy Council is a ceremonial "council of advisors" to the Queen. I know it sounds exhausting, but rest assured that no official duties go along with the distinction. In fact, Canadian privy councillors are required to do nothing.

Every former Canadian premier is a member, and the bottom line is that the Queen doesn't have Bob Rae on speed-dial. Membership is also open to anyone who is a good friend of the prime minister. For example, a previous Conservative government made Conrad Black a member of the Privy Council. It is somehow fitting that if Conrad goes down in a nasty prison brawl over a carton of cigarettes, the flag over the Peace Tower will fly at half mast.

Further down the list we come to "Senator." When a member of the Senate finally drops, the flag is not far behind. This has led to some confusion in the past when the flag has been lowered to half mast and it has turned out the senator in question was simply resting his eyes. As a result there is now a rigorous process to ensure the senator is actually deceased. Once death is established, the flag is immediately lowered.

Which brings us to the third category, a very interesting one indeed.

> on the death of a person whom it is desired to honour.

And rest assured the prime minister makes this call. The prime minister of Canada can order that flag lowered as a sign of respect to anyone we desire to honour. It is my suggestion that along with members of Parliament, senators and members of the Privy Council, we as a nation desire to honour men and women in uniform who pay the ultimate price while serving their country.

Prime Minister Harper, lower the flag.

IN BED WITH STEPHEN HARPER

It amazes me when I look back at the number of politicians who have been on the show and what some have them have agreed to do with the cameras rolling. It's easy to say that it's all about votes. There's no doubt that the prospect of few million eyeballs can go a long way when convincing a politician to appear on *RMR*. I've always described this phenomenon as a "mutually parasitic relationship": they need me, I need them, and more often than not when the cameras roll one of us has to close our eyes and think of the Queen. It's a tad more complicated than that, though. For a politician, being seen on TV doing something outside his or her comfort zone is never an easy call. It does take a certain amount of guts and risk.

To be honest, I never expected Stephen Harper, once he'd been elected prime minister, to heed any call, let alone the one that involved me sleeping over at 24 Sussex Drive. This is, after all, a man who can appear out of his comfort zone walking down a flight of steps or opening a door. And look—on the next couple of pages, for example—at some of the things I've said about him.

He did agree to appear, though. And once the cameras rolled he appeared pretty darn good. If there is a special place in hell for me as a result, I gladly accept my fate. There is no price too high to pay for a few good minutes of TV.

LYING DOWN WITH DOGS | OCT. 18, 2004

You've got to love a Liberal minority government. All the kids are back in school, but none of them can be sure who's going to be running the place from one minute to the next.

It's already pretty exciting. Parliament was back in session for five minutes before Stephen Harper jumped in bed with the Bloc Québécois and tried to defeat the government. I didn't see that coming. Sure, I thought they'd flirt with one another—chat each other up in the hallways. But they went straight past flirting and consummated that relationship right then and there in the leader of the opposition's office. I'm sure the desk was involved.

This was no quickie either. They were spoonin'. Harper was in there all cuddled up with Duceppe dreaming of throwing a Stampede breakfast at 24 Sussex Drive.

Call me old-fashioned, but when it comes to getting in bed with separatists for the sole purpose of defeating the government, I believe in abstinence.

Clearly Harper is more modern than I am when it comes to these things. Turns out that Harper will get in bed with anyone. I'm not saying anything, but the word is that Stephen Harper carried Jack Layton's books to school three times this week. Harper's not a Conservative, he's a tramp! You better be careful, Stephen—you can get a reputation for that kind of behaviour. One that can follow you through your entire four years of high school.

You know the expression: you lie down with dogs, you end up with fleas. You lie down with the Bloc and the NDP, God knows what you're going to get, but it's not going to help you in Alberta.

HARPER'S GAY PREOCCUPATION | JAN. 31, 2005

Conservative leader Stephen Harper is angry with the mainstream media and has every right to be, because it is the media that is trying to paint him as a man who cares more about same-sex marriage than any other issue. Which is just not fair.

Harper cares about other issues. He just doesn't know what they are yet. And just because he took out half-page ads about same-sex marriage and put them in papers all across the country does not mean that he's obsessed. Let's just says he's preoccupied. And sure, he could have taken out half-page ads and outlined his position on taxes or health care or education, but who can concentrate on issues like that when there's a couple of old lesbians in Lethbridge who want to get hitched?

And Harper has every right in the world to be angry at the media for implying that he's a leader who cares only about Alberta. Harper's own deputy leader, his right-hand man, is Peter MacKay from Nova Scotia. And sure, Harper never bothered to tell his deputy leader about the same-sex marriage ads, but that's because he's from Nova Scotia—he's different. It's like the Rat Pack: Sammy was allowed to sing with the group, but he wasn't allowed to help pick out the songs.

And finally, Harper must be pretty sick and tired of people saying that he's going tear up the Canadian Charter of Rights and Freedoms. That's just not true. He's just going to ignore the part about minorities.

And anyone who thinks otherwise . . . is gay.

SLEEPING OVER

24 Sussex Drive.
Broadcast Oct. 31, 2006

HARPER: Do the pyjamas fit?

MERCER: Yes, although I'm starting to feel a little compromised.

HARPER: Well, you look comfortable, and that's what we want.

SO YOU WANT TO BE A SPEECHWRITER?

JULY 17, 2005

Scott Feschuck is leaving his job as speechwriter in Prime Minister Paul Martin's office. This means that come the fall, we can look forward to a Martin who is even less amusing and less well spoken than usual. Hard to imagine, really. It also means that for the first time in decades, there is an actual job opening for a writer in Canada. Wherever writers gather, be it at book clubs, poetry circles, Narcotics Anonymous meetings or Margaret Atwood's house, this subject has dominated all others.

Personally, I think this represents a wonderful opportunity not only for professional writers, but for all unemployed Canadians.

Unlike most jobs, this one is a cinch to apply for: all letters to the prime minister of Canada are postage free.

If you are applying for the gig, you will have to provide a sample speech. Don't get carried away and attempt to write a Speech from the Throne. A Throne Speech outlines the government's priorities and its agenda. It's not the writer's job to decide the direction that the country is headed. That is sole responsibility of the director of communications.

So, what kind of speech? My advice is to put yourself in the shoes of the people around Paul Martin. Consider this: a newly released Strategic Counsel survey suggests 52 per cent of respondents believe the prime minister should be immediately replaced as leader of the Liberal party. Based on those numbers, it is safe to assume that those closest to him are looking for work elsewhere.

In light of the poll results, I'd say the smartest approach for any speechwriter candidate would be to craft a short but eloquent concession speech for the prime minister. Actually, I would write a speech for each of the two obvious scenarios: one to be used in the event of an election in which the Liberals get their asses kicked from sea to sea to sea, and another to be used in the event of a devastating result at a leadership review.

My professional advice—avoid clichés at all cost. For speech number one, the election night speech, I would start with something pithy and original, like:

My fellow Liberals—we are bloodied but we are unbowed! We may have lost official party status tonight, but we are still a force to be reckoned with! To Stephen Harper I say, congratulations, I'll be out of the house by Monday.

After that you would want to wrap it up pretty fast—the networks will have cut to Calgary by then anyway.

For the leadership review speech, I would start with a joke:

My fellow Liberals—I wish politics was like booze. Hey—27 per cent is a big number if you're talking alcohol content! [Pause for laughter.] Speaking of alcohol, I need a drink. Thank you and goodnight. Screw you, Ignatieff!

My only other advice is to keep it short. Nobody likes a long-winded prime minister. (If you get the job, good luck getting that message through his head.)

Send all applications to:

I Want to Be a Speechwriter
c/o Office of the Prime Minister
80 Wellington Street
Ottawa K1A 0A2

P.S. Remember when corresponding with any member of Parliament to sign off by asking to be added to his or her Christmas-card list. This way, when December rolls around, you will know if anyone bothered to read your letter.

ELECTION FEVER

Very early in the great campaign of 2005 the two big parties made their election strategies pretty clear. The Tories were going to hammer away at the Liberals as corrupt, venal, and unworthy of governing—which, you have to admit, was a pretty good plan. The Liberals, however, decided to take the high road. They decided that their best chance of winning was to convince Canadians that Liberal values were Canadian values. And how were they going to do that? By bribing us.

FROM THE DESK OF PRIME MINISTER MARTIN | NOV. 29, 2005

Hello, fellow Liberals, and Merry Elexmas one and all.

Wow! Can you believe it's Holiday Newsletter time again?

As you know, today the governor general dissolved the 38th Parliament of Canada. It seems like barely eighteen months ago we were celebrating the birth of our recently deceased minority government. Well, I guess we weren't so much "celebrating" as putting a brave face on. Whatever you call it, there was drinking involved.

I find it hard to discuss the 38th Parliament. All I can say is that, like you, I once had high hopes for its future. Needless to say, it was devastating to me personally when I finally realized that the 38th Parliament of Canada—the fruit of my loins, as it were—was hopelessly retarded. Sorry, developmentally delayed.

Once the initial shock wore off, I decided that the only decent thing to do was to play the hand I was dealt. Turned out in the end that no amount of money could save the bloody thing, and twenty billion dollars later Stephen Harper took it on himself to put the poor simp out of its misery.

So here we are.

So much has happened since that last election, so I'll try to be brief. Phase one of the Gomery Report came out, and I have been completely vindicated. Turns out I had no idea what was going on. Some people find this hard to believe, but to those naysayers I say, think back to high school. Remember that dim kid you hung out with in grade ten who never had a frigging clue what was happening? Remember him? That's basically me, except I'm far more powerful. This is the case I will bring forward to Canada.

I'm pleased to report that the democratic deficit has been all but eliminated. *Kidding!* It's screwed, but what's a guy to do? I have Belinda on the file and she says it's under control, and that's good enough for me.

Of course I have to mention Belinda. If it wasn't for her, this government would have died months ago, and me along with it. Some people in the press have referred to her as my guardian angel. I prefer to think of her as my political defibrillator. Even to this day, when I see her coming I want to tear open my shirt, put Vaseline on my nipples and yell, *Clear!*

The rest of the front bench is doing well and looking forward to the coming Elexmas season.

I am proud to report that Deputy Prime Minister Anne McLellan is raring to go. People don't know how hard she works. I bumped into her just minutes after the non-confidence vote and instead of feeling sorry for us, she was busy putting up posters for a yard sale at her house. Everything must go, apparently. She is a multi-tasker, that Anne!

Scott Brison has turned out to be the star of the front bench. I am sick and tired of people saying that the behaviour in Question Period is like a bunch of kids on the playground. If it was like a playground, would I hide behind the gay kid when I got picked on? Hardly.

Anyway, I have to go now. Scott Reid is barking at me to get my ass in his office pronto! May I take this time as your prime minister to wish you well, and may I be the first to say to you: Merry Elexmas, and let's hope we live to see another year.

Sincerely,
Paul Martin

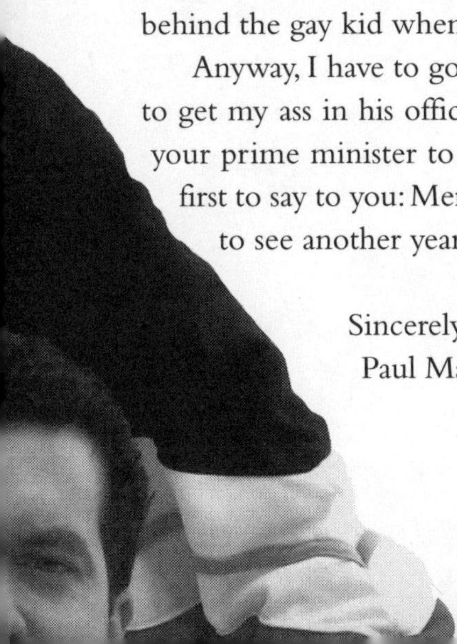

FROM THE DESK OF STEPHEN HARPER | NOV. 30, 2005

My fellow Conservatives,

It has come to my attention that the lying Liberals have recently released an "Elexmas newsletter" that is nothing but a further example of the culture of entitlement. I would like to take this opportunity to emulate them. Let us never forget, as Conservatives, that we despise the Liberals and all they stand for and that there must be no discernable difference between us and them.

So, Merry Elexmas!

By now you know that we have defeated the government. It has been suggested that the people of Canada do not want an election at this juncture. Those of you who know me know this: I don't care what the people think. I am not a people person. I don't like people, and the feeling is mutual.

I am sick of this discussion. I ask you, why in heaven's name would I like people? The so-called people had their chance eighteen months ago, and they chose not to give me a majority. This morning I suggested to Tom Flanagan that we change our campaign slogan from "Standing up for Canada" to "Screw the People." He said no, pointing out that in politics honesty is not the best policy. "Besides," he added, "300 million bucks on an election nobody wants is about as big a 'screw you' to the people as the Tories can muster." How we laughed!

So far I feel the campaign is going really well. In an effort to appease Ontario voters, it is imperative that we bring forward an image of moderation. To this end, I would like to point out that I waited a full five hours after Parliament was dissolved before I started in on the queers.

Some leftists have suggested that I chose the first day of the campaign to discuss gay marriage so as to get the issue out of the way. This is not true. I chose to discuss gay marriage on day one because it is a number-one issue. In fact I would like nothing better than to spend every day of this campaign discussing gay sex. Unfortunately I cannot do that, but I am announcing today the formation of a Conservative gay sex caucus. The caucus will meet with me throughout the campaign and will monitor any new gay sex practices that may develop over the holiday season.

As you know, I have stated that when I am prime minister I will hold a free vote in Parliament on the issue of gay marriage. And let me reiterate: "I will not whip my cabinet on the issue of same-sex marriage." When I made that commitment to caucus Jason Kenney broke the ice by raising his hand and saying, "Whip me! Whip me!" What a soldier! Later he pulled me aside at John Baird's headquarters and told me sincerely that if asked to sit in cabinet, he will serve, and that he for one will gladly be whipped on the issue of gay marriage. He is a stand-up guy, Jason, always willing to subjugate himself for the cause of Conservatism.

Anyway, it's day two and I have to run. Somebody at Tory headquarters gave my phone number to Peter MacKay, and now I have to get a new number and initiate another purge.

Good luck and God bless,
Stephen Harper

IT WON'T WORK THIS TIME | NOV. 29, 2005

Bribery—that's what we value, apparently. We value being bought off with our own money. And we're not talking chump change here, either. The Liberals dropped between twenty and thirty billion dollars of our own money on the way out the door. But, you know, I don't think it's going to work this time. Canadians know how this game is played. If the Liberals were serious about bribing us, they would have sent us all one of those big Liberal envelopes stuffed full of cash we've heard so much about. And if they were really serious about making an impression, they would have had the envelopes delivered in style—by, say, Belinda Stronach on horseback in the rain without a saddle. That's how you win a majority.

But barring that, wouldn't it be nice if this was a campaign of ideas? Because so far, we've heard none. In fact, this is not a campaign, this is a case of déjà vu. The Liberals are going to accuse the Tories of having a hidden agenda. To which the Tories will say, "No, no, no, we don't have a hidden agenda. We've just kept our election campaign platform a secret for six months because we're afraid someone will steal it."

They say the definition of insanity is doing the same thing over and over again and expecting a different result. Tragically, that's also the definition of politics in Canada.

MOST EXCITING NIGHT | JAN. 23, 2006

I can't help myself—every election night I'm like a kid at Christmas. Except this time it's way worse. I'm like a kid with ADHD at Christmas who just ate a great big bag of white sugar. And can you blame me? This election night is shaping up to be one of the most exciting nights in Canadian history.

Nobody knows what's going to happen. It could be a minority, a majority, a coalition government, a separatist opposition—nobody knows. All we know is that whatever we end up with, it's going to be really strange and there's no guarantee it will survive.

It's a bit like that time of year when the American networks roll out their big new comedy pilots. If the NDP does well tonight, this time tomorrow the most powerful man in Canada could be a tiny socialist with a gay moustache. Likewise, if the Tories take it, in a week to ten days Stockwell Day could be getting sworn in as Canada's minister of foreign affairs. Now personally, I don't think that's going to happen. Mainly because I'm not that lucky.

And of course there's always the chance that the Liberals can hang on and form another Liberal minority government. In which case all of Canada will wake up tomorrow—or at least its 24 million voters will—and say, "Wow, next time why don't we save ourselves 250 million bucks? We'll pick a date, we'll get together and smack ourselves in the head with a hammer and we'll get the same results."

Yes, it's quite a country. But you know, no matter what kind of weird, wonderful or only-in-Canada kind of government we end up with, we all had the opportunity to vote, we all got to have our say, and not a single shot was fired. That, my friends, is a country worth voting for.

SO LONG, SO-CONS | OCT. 2, 2007

Once again Ottawa is red-hot with election fever.

Now of course, I'd love an election. For me, an election's like the World Series. I'd take one every October. But in fact, if there is an election coming up, it's going to be a truly interesting one. It will be historic. For the first time ever, we'd have a Liberal party that has no idea what it is or what it stands for versus a Conservative party that's suddenly decided it's no longer conservative but big-tax-and-spend liberal.

But more importantly, for the first time in a very long time we are going to have an election where the so-cons, those good, God-fearing, very politically active social conservatives, are going to have absolutely no influence or say on the debate or the agenda. It's like we woke up in Fidel Castro's Cuba.

We have Stephen Harper to thank for this. Because since he became prime minister it's like he's managed to successfully spay and neuter every single one of those so-cons. Think about this. If social conservatives in this country were animals, of the four-legged variety, they'd be on some form of endangered species list. Cripes, if they had gills, David Suzuki would have to organize an emergency round table on how to protect them. As it stands now, the only evidence that the so-cons actually exist is when you talk to Tories and they laugh their asses off about how much money these people keep sending the party.

Now there is a very clever trick. Imagine convincing thousands of people to send you millions of dollars so you can form a government. Then you form the government and as a reward to those people you tell them to shut up and forget everything they've ever stood for and then you give them nothing. And then they send you more money in return because they have nowhere else to go. Whoever said Stephen Harper is a brilliant strategist wasn't lying.

So if we're heading into a federal election where Stephen Harper might form a majority, there are only two explanations: the social conservatives have been sold down a river, or they know something we don't.

CHOOSING THE NERD

As much as I love an election, I love a leadership convention even more. From a showbiz perspective politics doesn't get much better than this. In an election the parties turn on each other; in a leadership convention a party turns on itself. This leads to a whole new level of carnage and destruction. Being a well-lubricated fly on the wall at one of these family feuds is just too much fun.

The Liberal leadership convention in Montreal was the most fun I had in all of 2006. And given the result, I don't think there'll ever be another one like it. Some things, like choosing a leader for example, are simply too important to be trusted to delegates.

blackberry

FLIGHT DELAYED | DEC. 1, 2006

I am not in Montreal for the Liberal leadership convention. I am sitting on the tarmac in Toronto. Air Canada delayed my flight three times, and I have just boarded my flight almost two hours behind schedule.

Earlier tonight I caught Joe Volpe's speech on TV. Volpe's introduction video was put together by the same children who donated money to his campaign. It wasn't even a video, actually, it was just a collection of old pictures of Joe set to Tom Cochrane's *Life Is a Highway*. It didn't seem like a campaign video so much as the type of thing well-meaning but talentless children might prepare for their parents' fiftieth wedding anniversary. Usually these things work because family members get to laugh at the bad hairstyles from the seventies. I think the purpose here was to make people think, "Wow, Joe has been to the Great Wall of China—he should be our leader."

The Iggy and Bob speeches I watched at the airport. Not a bad place to watch, really. I was in a similar situation years ago when I joined the huddle around an airport television to watch the Canadian women's hockey team win the gold. This time it wasn't nearly as hard to get a seat with a decent view.

One guy who was pretty knackered announced to those watching that Bob Rae looked "familiar"; this got a pretty good laugh. A few minutes later he announced, "I think he's a comedian." Bob certainly exhibited a stand-up's confidence by leaving the safety of the podium and walking to the edge of the stage. At the halfway point, when Bob made the joke about Harper's cabinet being vegetables, the guy laughed a little too hard and said, "See? He's funny!"

Ignatieff, I noticed, speaks very slowly—the sign of a good educator. He wants to make sure that even the dim kids can follow him. I admit I have a problem with this style. When Iggy starts waving that bloody finger around, I feel like I'm back in Ms. Patzold's grade eight class. His legions of fans seemed to like it, though. When he wiggles the finger they tingle inside. I think Iggy actually made a big mistake and either reached into the wrong pocket or ticked off the TelePrompter guy because it seemed to me that he was delivering his victory speech. I remember thinking it had something to do with "hope." Basically he decided to do Bill Clinton's act but not as well.

Air Canada is "looking for a pilot." It's going to be a long night, but not the kind I had envisioned.

THE MORNING AFTER | DEC. 2, 2006

The one advantage of showing up to a party stone cold sober at 1:50 a.m. is that you will probably be the only one who remembers anything. The disadvantage this time was that by the time I arrived at ground zero, the delegates were drunk and confident—a bad combination.

The Delta Hotel lobby was a zoo just a few hours ago. Hundreds of young people were circling like parched animals in search of a watering hole. There was no shortage of options—on the way to the elevator I was told that there were free shots in a Dryden room and a huge Dion event happening, with a free ice vodka fountain. I kind of felt nostalgic for the days when I would have walked over broken glass to reach such a Shangri-La. I ended up having a few Heinekens in a room that apparently was rented by Paul Martin. Martin wasn't there, but it seems the huge podium in the corner is one he practises on when preparing for a big speech.

There are two schools of thought on Ignatieff's early-round results: it's possible that Ignatieff's people intentionally suppressed a pile of votes on the first ballot, knowing they will come to him on the second. This is an old trick that guarantees that there will be growth on the second ballot, which gives the illusion of momentum.

My gut tells me this is not what happened. I talked to one Iggy delegate last night who was vicious because he saw three Iggy ballots destroyed and on the floor in the voting area. He seemed to think there was some sort of conspiracy afoot. I figure that those three ballots belonged either to people who were too stupid to get them in the slot or to people who couldn't bring themselves to do what they promised to do months ago.

I just watched Iggy get cornered by CBC's Julie Van Dusen. She asked what his reaction was to the first-round results. Iggy said that his first-round results were lower than expected because he spoke last, which meant some of his delegates didn't get a chance to vote.

If that's the best line the Iggy brain trust can come up with, that camp is in serious trouble.

PALAIS DE CONGRÈS: SECOND BALLOT

Iggy looks visibly shaken. I think he should compose himself and take this moment to reflect and enjoy the experience. After all, after this vote it will be a long time before he sees his name on a ballot again (barring, of course, the annual sexiest professor poll at Harvard—his name goes on that ballot the minute he signs his new contract). It's times like this that a candidate should show grace under pressure, and I think it was beneath Iggy to accuse Gerard Kennedy of committing a war crime by throwing his support to Dion.

The Ignatieff delegates I've been talking to have that tragic air of someone in palliative care eating applesauce and making big plans to run a marathon.

It's understandable that the Ignatieff people are having a hard time dealing with this; they felt that Iggy's actually winning this thing was just a technicality. Now they are willing to grasp at any straw available. Soon after the second-ballot results came in, an Ignatieff delegate grabbed me and waved his BlackBerry in my face and shouted, "Dryden is about to announce he's supporting Iggy." The words were not out of his mouth before another delegate started waving his BlackBerry around and shouting, "Dryden went to Rae."

In this room, if you wave your BlackBerry as you speak it carries the same weight as waving a Bible at an evangelical conference. It's in the good BlackBerry—it must be true!

The only guy having a good day at this point is soon-to-be leader of the opposition Stéphane Dion.

FOURTH BALLOT

Before the results were announced, my friend Mike and I spent twenty minutes working our way to the middle of the room so we could be surrounded by a mix of Dion and Ignatieff supporters.

It was tightly packed there. Looking around and seeing the desperate look on everyone's faces reminded me of the Ayatollah's funeral. I was happy to observe all weekend, but at this moment I really felt like an interloper. This was their party, and they had invested everything in it. For these people the stakes don't get any higher.

When the results were finally announced and it was immediately clear that Dion had stolen the race from Ignatieff, people all around us basically melted. To the right of me a guy with a Dion bandanna around his neck burst into tears and started cheering like peace on earth had been declared. On the other side of me there were tears as well, but the other kind.

Michael Ignatieff was gracious in defeat. It's pretty ironic that this experience, which has to rank up there as a personal worst for him, may in fact have been his finest moment in public life.

Dion's victory speech was very good, but all it really did was confirm everyone's preconceived notions of the guy. Liberals see a saviour who will bring them back to power, and the Tories are rubbing their hands in glee over the prospect of heading into battle against a French guy who has a dog named Kyoto. Dion is an enigma to most Canadians, and that's not such a bad thing. He takes over the Liberal party as a relative unknown, and as a result, people have pretty low expectations of him. This is a good position for a politician to be in; he has nowhere to go but up.

At the end of the day, though, watching Dion on stage, I couldn't help but be amazed at his physical presence. The Liberals went into this convention with a host of choices. They could have gone with a battle-tested politician, a former athlete, a world-famous academic or a food-bank founder from the west; at the end of the day they chose the nerd. That's pretty Canadian.

DOGGING DION

In Montreal with Stéphane Dion and Kyoto. Broadcast Jan. 9, 2007

MERCER: And here we are with the most famous dog in Canada now—Kyoto. How long have you had Kyoto?

DION: We chose to have a dog last January, after the defeat. Because we knew that the Conservatives would not be very good about planet change, we thought that a dog of the north, the Arctic, would be a good choice, a kind of symbol for us. And we called the dog Kyoto indeed for that.

MERCER: And did Stephen Harper neuter him?

KYOTO: *Whimper.*

THAT OTHER GUY, AGAIN

TALIBAN JACK | JAN. 16, 2007

So the NDP gathered in British Columbia this past week for their annual national caucus retreat. Traditionally, when the big parties get together like this, it's a time to roll up their sleeves and make big plans for the future. Now, of course I have no idea what went on behind the closed doors, but I think if the NDP are making plans for the future, they might want to look into the concept of a prearranged funeral. Because that smell that's coming out of their caucus room, that's an electrical fire in Jack Layton's head.

The prognosis is not good. They're in serious trouble, they are tanking in the polls, and so far the only way they can figure out how to survive is if the NDP props up the Conservative budget. Which is kind of like being told that if you really want that new kidney, you're going to have to give up your lungs. It's desperate. They can't even make the issue of the environment work for them. Meanwhile, the new leader of the Liberal party's out there running around, and he's wearing so much green he's looking like some sort of demented Keebler elf. And then when poor old Jack tries to talk about any other issues at all, Canadians basically just point at him and they laugh. Like when he suggested that Canada should be sponsoring peace talks with the Taliban.

Ah, that was a really good idea. Especially if you think "Taliban Jack" is the name that should be ringing in people's heads as they head into an election. Now to be fair, Taliban Jack did say that as long as the troops were at war, he would stand behind them. Which I'm assuming is only because it's a lot safer than standing in front of the troops. Although the way things are going now, I would say his odds of surviving that, or a general election, are pretty much the same.

THE RISE AND STUMBLE OF STÉPHANE DION

Canadians love to root for an underdog and the Liberals showed their true Canadian colours in the way the voting went that December. Stéphane Dion was the underdog from the moment he launched his campaign, and the fact that he pulled off a fourth-ballot victory against the establishment front-runner was nothing short of miraculous.

What followed was a little less amazing.

NOT AGAIN | JAN. 30, 2007

If you talk to the crowd in Ottawa these days, whether they're Liberals or they're Tories, they're all gearing up for another election and that's exactly the way they like it.

Now personally, I can't believe this is actually happening. The Conservative government is just twelve months old. The Liberal government it replaced was just eighteen months old. I've got a box of baking soda in my fridge that's now older than two consecutive governments. And yet there's Harper and Dion, chomping at the bit ready to go to the polls. And why? Because that's what they do. They can't stop themselves. They're like sled dogs: their brains are wired for one thing and one thing only, and that is running. They'll stop occasionally to lick themselves or to put their stamp on the Ministry of Public Works, but other than that it's all about running with these guys.

Harper I understand. The man wants a majority so bad he can taste it. And he doesn't care if Canadians have to suffer through another election so he can get one.

But for the life of me I can't see why Stéphane Dion would want another election. For starters, nobody knows anything about this guy. The Liberals just had their big retreat in Quebec City. As far as I can tell the only thing that came out of that was that Dion got a new haircut and he's still upset about Kyoto. Stéphane, would it kill you to talk about something else for two minutes?

Last week the minister of defence came out and said the real reason he thinks we're in Afghanistan is as an act of retribution for the attacks on the twin towers. And the Liberals, they just sat there like a bunch of slack-jawed yokels.

Stéphane, here's a little tip. When the minister of defence publicly contradicts everything the prime minister has ever said about why we are in an actual war, you might want to send out a press release. Maybe that's not the day to talk about polar bears.

Until you get your act together, Stéphane, let's just hold off going into an election. Because Canadians, whether you like it or not, look at governments just like we look at that box of baking soda. We get a new one, we slap it in the back of the fridge, we forget about it. We don't even think about changing it until it starts to smell.

INSULTING OUR INTELLIGENCE | FEB. 6, 2007

Like most Canadians, when I see a glaring difference between American and Canadian culture, I like it when Canada has the edge. But it doesn't always work out that way. Take the Super Bowl commercials, for example. In the United States, millions of people gather to watch the Super Bowl, but also to watch the flashy new commercials. And then after the game, guys sit around and talk about the game, and about the size of the hooters on that girl in the Doritos ad. That's America for you.

In Canada things are a little bit different. In Canada, the only time they actually talk about commercials on the news is when the Tories launch a series of attack ads on the Liberals out of the blue.

Now, don't get me wrong, Stéphane Dion looks pretty sexy in those ads, what with his nice glasses and all. And personally I'm glad that the attack ads have started. I find it refreshing to see a prime minister give up that whole "dignity of the office" routine and devote a big chunk of his time on the job to campaigning in a campaign that apparently doesn't even exist. What upsets me is how wimpy everyone's acting. The election hasn't even been called yet and already everyone's saying their feelings are hurt.

There's no room for feelings in politics. The Liberals are upset because Harper says Dion is not a leader and the Tories are upset because Dion called Harper overweight. This is shaping up to be a real intellectual battle of the Titans, isn't it? You got one guy saying, "You're not the boss of me" and the other guy coming back with, "Oh yeah—you're fat." I had better debates with my brother in grade three.

Unless these two guys start talking about some real issues and acting their age, come election day voters might decide to take a pass on both of them, pull the car over, reach into the back seat and just knock their two heads together.

NEGATIVE MOMENTUM | MAR. 13, 2007

The Liberal leadership race was one of the longest in Canadian history, and by the looks of it, it's about to get a heck of a lot longer. Because there's no doubt about it, the knives are out for Stéphane Dion.

Now I have no idea what happened at that convention in Montreal, but I'm startin' to think that Dion might have spiked the Kool-Aid, because here it is, three months later, it's only dawning on the Liberals now that they went out and picked the guy that can't really communicate.

Watching this guy in action, and I use the word "action" very loosely, I can't even figure out why he wanted the job in the first place. He acts like some dude who didn't come to work one day and while he was away all the boys got together and had him elected shop steward. And this past week, in an effort to turn all this negative momentum around, he's been out there on the road talking to supporters in intimate settings, because apparently that's where he does his best work.

Wow, talk about a great communication strategy, Stéphane. Show up in a Legion hall in Flin Flon, spend an hour talking about yourself in front of sixty-five locals—keep that up and in about two thousand years you might form a minority.

Now, of course Stéphane says he just wants to reach out and touch the grassroots—which is ironic, because at this point the grassroots wants to reach out and give him a smack in the head. So basically, the situation for the Liberal party is pretty clear. They went out and elected a leader who can't talk, and Canadians aren't that interested in what he has to say.

Other than that—things are pretty good. Especially if your name is Bob Rae or Michael Ignatieff.

ON COURSE WITH ANNE MURRAY

Lakeland, Florida.
Broadcast Mar. 11, 2008

MERCER: OK—what do I need?

MURRAY: Well, you should start with probably a pitching wedge or a nine iron, just to get warmed up.

MERCER: I don't need to warm up. I want the big thing . . .

[*Sounds of commotion nearby.*]

MURRAY: Wow . . .

Mercer: Is there gonna be a fight?

MURRAY: Somebody hit that 50-yard sign—

MERCER: —Oh, and it bounced back? Wow. I thought we were gonna see a brawl there for a second. But you would have had my back, right, if people started swinging fists? That's good. 'Cause I get nervous in a fight.

MURRAY: No wonder. Anyone who wears that hat should be nervous.

DOING SOMETHING RIGHT FOR A CHANGE

I know we've produced a good show when I get five emails from Tories accusing me of being a Liberal shill and five emails from Liberals accusing me of being a Tory. Usually there also are a few from the NDP asking why I ignore them all the time, but that's beside the point.

It's easier to criticize the people who run the country than it is to praise them, of course. And usually better deserved. Occasionally, however, it's nice to step back from the partisan posturing and give credit where credit is due.

HARPER IN GHANNI | MAR. 14, 2006

Stephen Harper wasn't kidding when he promised that he was going to govern differently. Compared to previous prime ministers, "different" is an understatement.

For starters, he takes the concept of stand-offish to a whole new level. It's like the morning after the campaign he woke up and said, "Wow. Thank God that's over. Now I can go back to being creeped out by people." Then he just disappeared. He went up to his office and locked himself away.

Now of course, this freaks the media out, because they're not used to it. Compared to, say, Mulroney or Chrétien, Harper's agoraphobic. He's like a crazy old lady with nine cats. But you've got to give him credit. When he comes out of hiding, he does it with a bang.

Popping up out of the blue in Afghanistan was very impressive. Because it is one thing for a prime minister to stand up in the lobby of the House of Commons and say nice things about our men and women in uniform, but anyone can do that. That move is on page one of the idiot's guide to being a prime minister. But for Harper to actually go to Afghanistan in person, that was putting his money where his mouth is.

Kandahar is a snakepit no matter who you are. And for him to go there in person, it was telling those twenty-three hundred Canadian soldiers—who are risking their lives every single day—that if it's good enough for them, it's good enough for the prime minister. We're all in this together.

That speech is worth a thousand speeches on Canadian soil. Because of that one visit, twenty-three hundred troops now know that the new guy has their back. And the rest of us know he's capable of the occasional classy move.

HARPER AND CHINA | NOV. 21, 2006

There's no doubt about it, the major economic superpower on the block these days is China. So it's no surprise that a lot of people freaked out when they heard that the president of China wouldn't even meet with Harper at the APEC Summit. But before anyone starts to think that Harper's screwed up one of the most important economic relationships that Canada has, let's be clear on one thing: it was the president of China who asked Harper out in the first place, and then when Harper said yes, China said no and then they said yes again.

It's like China asked Harper out on an Internet date but then changed its mind once he showed up and didn't look like his picture. *Hey, that's no swimmer's build!* Then when China realized how shallow it would look, it agreed to a date, but drinks, no dinner. Clearly, China is a very fickle mistress.

Now, to be fair, the Liberals were masters at this relationship. Chrétien spent more time in Beijing than he ever spent in Alberta. But that was then, this is now, and Canada is definitely off China's Christmas list. Not that Christmas is legal in China—but you get my point. And so what has the Harper government done that was so bad? Believe it or not, they've been too critical of China on human rights.

Basically, a bunch of Tories went off to Vancouver and met the Dalai Lama, and China went crazy. And you know what? Who cares? Last time I looked, Canada was a free country. And the Chinese economy can grow as fast as it wants to, but that does not change the fact that we can meet with whomever we want. We can worship who we want, vote for who we want. Heck, for the time being we can even go out and get married to who we want.

So China's little hissy fit is their problem, not ours. And sure we'll do business with China, but we're not going to act like China. Harper has done nothing wrong here; in fact, when it comes to China, for the first time in a long time, Canada's done something right.

MY DINNER WITH STEVEN | AUG. 8, 2005

Steven Fletcher rolled into town this week for the caucus retreat, and we finally followed through with an ongoing threat to hook up and have a few beers. Actually, it turns out he doesn't drink beer, but luckily he doesn't mind buying it.

Fletcher is one of my favourite Tories. He is the health critic, a very funny guy and a great interview. He's also up for anything, which I love in an MP. The first time I interviewed him we tied a rope to the back of his wheelchair, I got on a Razor and he towed me around the Parliament buildings at a very alarming speed.

There are certain advantages when shooting a segment on Parliament Hill with a quadriplegic. Normally if I tried to use a scooter on the Hill I'd be bounced in about three seconds. If you happen to be with a guy in a wheelchair, everyone assumes it's on the up and up. Steven is well aware of this advantage. Rumour has it that as a party trick he will intentionally run into a Liberal so that everyone gets to watch as the Liberal apologizes for being in the way.

After two Heinekens at Stephen Fletcher's hotel we walked/motored up to Queen Street to Le Select Bistro for steak frites. In honour of my Western-based Conservative friend, I thought a French bistro was only appropriate.

I felt flattered to have been fitted into his diary. If anyone ever gets it in their head that MPs don't work like Torbay ponies in the summer, they should check out Fletcher's schedule. He has toured over twenty-five hospitals in Ontario alone this summer, and has plans to see more. He is totally obsessed with his portfolio. He can talk health care until your eyes cross.

And nice? This is a guy who has absolutely no anger in his voice when he tells the very funny story about an airline losing his wheelchair.

Not long ago he found himself in Ottawa, sitting on a plane at 1:00 a.m., having just flown all the way from Winnipeg through Toronto, and nobody had a sweet clue where his wheelchair was. Eventually he ended up spending the night lying on an air mattress in the chapel. He literally had to stay there until the next day so they could find the lost chair and fly it to Ottawa. And just when you think the story has ended he gets to the part about how the chapel filled up at dawn with travellers of the Muslim faith who had to take part in the Muslim call to prayer. Luckily they didn't mind the guy lying on the air mattress in the middle of the room, and Steven is partial to chanting.

It's a funny story, but he's a better man than I.

I go shit-crazy if my luggage stays on the tarmac for longer than thirty minutes. This guy's wheelchair gets lost and he is Mr. These Things Happen.

And just to be clear, I don't mean to imply he isn't capable of anger. When he talks about the Gomery Inquiry, he looks like his head is going to come off his shoulders. He seems to have a huge tolerance for an honest mistake and an extremely low tolerance for graft and corruption. Not surprising, really. It's probably proof of his Conservative hidden agenda.

BLAME GAME | FEB. 20, 2007

Blaming the government for all our troubles is a great Canadian pastime. And I admit I've been doing that for much of my natural life. But occasionally the government gets the stick for something over which it has no control. And more often than not, when it happens, it's courtesy of Canada's all-knowing auditor general, Sheila Fraser.

Fraser, apparently, has the power and the authority of the Pope, the Queen and the Dalai Lama all wrapped up in one. If this woman gets any more powerful, one of these days Canadians are going to wake up and find her standing at the foot of our beds yelling at us because our socks are on the floor.

Sheila's currently upset about the Passport Office. Apparently they didn't have a plan in place to deal with all the Canadians who suddenly want to travel to the United States but don't have a passport.

I know it sucks to be stuck in a lineup—I would rather have a spinal tap—but how in God's name is this the government's fault? Because unless you've been living in a tin, we all knew this was happening. The Liberals warned us about this two years ago. And I'm sorry, if it's seven o'clock on Christmas Eve and you're stuck at the back of a lineup with four hundred guys and a Tickle Me Elmo doll, that's your fault, not Wal-Mart's.

I know, it's a tragedy that Dylan and Dougie want to spend March break at the Girls Gone Wild beach bash in Daytona Beach and they just figured today that's not in Ontario, but that is hardly a national crisis. Other than rounding us all up at gunpoint and forcing us into the Passport Office, I don't think there's much more the government can do on this.

No matter what Sheila Fraser thinks, you cannot legislate against leaving things to the last minute. Which is a good thing—because otherwise, like most Canadians, I would be in jail.

A FEW MODEST PROPOSALS

Like I said earlier, it's a lot easier to criticize the people who run our country than it is to sing their praises. Constructive suggestions tend not to come so readily either. But once in a while I do find myself trying to be a bit more helpful.

IT'S HEALTH, STUPID | MAR. 22, 2004

Everyone is talking about how Paul Martin could lose the next election. Which, let's face it, is very Canadian. Sure we love our winners. We just don't mind when our winners suddenly take a face plant on the wrong side of the finish line. It's just something in our nature.

And you have to admit, this is a very sexy story. There he is, Paul Martin, a man like any other man, except for some reason he is obsessed with becoming the prime minister of Canada. Why? Who knows, he just is. And then, after a lifetime of dedication, he finally gets the job only to see it all go horribly wrong and end in a humiliating defeat. It's like something right out of the Old Testament.

Things are not good for the Liberals right now. For the first time in a decade, they actually have an opposition. And this whole sponsorship scandal, no matter how you look at it, makes them look like they've been stealing from the taxpayer. In terms of optics, stealing from the taxpayer is never very good.

But as much as Canadians want to punish the Liberals, they might give them another chance. If, that is, they come through on health care. Look at the polls, Paul. Health care is all Canadians are concerned about. And I know why, too. It's the baby boomers again. They can't walk to the corner store without blowing out their knees, so they want the system fixed, and they want it fixed now.

Yes, a health care budget could turn it around for the Liberals. And Paul, this doesn't mean having someone stand up in the House of Commons and say, "Health care is a Liberal priority." That ain't gonna work. For that to work, people would have to trust the Liberals, and they don't anymore. They might vote for you, but they definitely don't trust you.

People want to see cash in the system. We want to see happy nurses, happy doctors, happy premiers. Come on, Paul, health care could be your ace in the hole, but talking about it is not going to do it. You want to keep your job, you're going to have to put your money where your mouth is. So remove the foot and show us the cash.

PAUL MARTIN'S ARMY | JAN. 12, 2004

Canada's defence policy is very simple: we don't really need one because America's defence policy is also very simple. Basically, if you mess with America, they will kill you.

Because we're attached to America, nobody messes with us. We're like the cockiest kid in grade three. Nobody in the playground is going to say boo to us because we've got a brother who's in grade six, weighs two hundred pounds and can break stuff with his forehead.

If that's the case, why do we have the Armed Forces in the first place? Well, obviously, Ottawa's been wondering the same thing. Prime Minister Martin was minister of finance for ten years. He used to make cuts to the military before his feet hit the floor in the morning, but did that mean fewer missions? No, it meant more missions with fewer resources, which would lead to the equipment debate. Ottawa would say the Armed Forces have all the equipment they need, whereas the guys getting shot at would say, um, no, actually we don't.

So who are you going to believe? I have no idea, but I do have a proposal, and I think Paul Martin will like it because it's fiscally responsible, and he gets off on that sort of thing.

This is my plan. For the next ten years, when it comes to the Armed Forces, we spend like drunken sailors. I don't know where the money's going to come from. We can put it on the Canadian Tire card for all I care. But if the Armed Forces say they need something, we give it to them. And then in 2013, we can sit down and we can say, okay, we've got these excellent, fully equipped Armed Forces. Are we going to keep going with this peacekeeping thing, this idea that we came up with that defined us all over the world, or are we just going to say, shag it, let's close the entire works down, have a yard sale, shut up and go sit at the kiddie table with Iceland?

I know, Paul, it's an expensive plan. But if we're going to ask people to leave the best place on earth and go to the worst places on earth and keep the peace and do it in the name of Canada, the least we can do is back them up with the gold card.

CHILDREN ARE THE FUTURE BUT BEER IS NOW | DEC. 13, 2005

Like so many Canadians, I was appalled by Scott Reid's comment about the proposed Conservative child care plan. In case you missed it, Scott recently quipped that under the plan parents could choose to spend their twenty-five-dollar-a-week child care allowance on beer instead of child care. Clearly Scott is wrong. We all know that in this country it would be impossible to find a parent who would spend twenty-five bucks a week on beer. For starters, a case of beer costs more than twenty-five bucks. A case of domestic is about thirty-five bucks, and the trendier imports cost even more. I happen to know this because I drink beer. I don't have kids, so I had no idea what child care costs. I admit I'm surprised to discover that twenty-five bucks a week will cover it, but what do I know.

While we all recognize and agree that Scott is an enemy of all that is holy, I feel there is a bigger issue at hand here. In the stampede to condemn Scott and his comments about child care policy, I have noticed a very real and very ugly sentiment sneaking into the national discourse. I am talking of course, about an anti-beer agenda.

I ask you, Canada, since when is it okay to beat up beer drinkers?

I do not believe that just because someone said something stupid it should suddenly be open season on lovers of ale and lager. We all have a responsibility to protect the most vulnerable in society, and this week the most vulnerable are the people you have a few pints with.

So I ask you: who will stand up for the beer drinker? Not the Conservative party, that's for sure. The Conservative party has made statements about beer this week that are not just hurtful but verge on the hateful.

Conservative child care critic Rona Ambrose called a press conference this week to condemn Scott Reid. That's fine, but did she stop there? No. Rona Ambrose placed a warm case of Blue on a table and openly mocked both the product and those who consume it.

She held a case of Blue up for ridicule! Is this a

Canada you recognize? Imagine if she did this with a Jewish person or a homosexual or a midget! Shame, Rona, shame.

And now I hear that an "anti-beer special interest group" has created a website to promote this anti-beer, pro-child agenda. They are collecting names for a petition at the website www.kidsnotbeer.com.

I am not prepared to let the Kids Not Beer people win this one. I know these people have a healthy head start, but beer drinkers are out there, and if I can get to them before six or seven in the evening, they can be organized. Together we can stand up and say, "My Canada includes having a few pops."

So please go to www.beernotkids.com and sign my Beer Not Kids petition.

Let's stop the hate and let the beer drinking begin.

Remember: children may be our greatest resource, but beer is our greatest beverage.

And besides, if it wasn't for beer most of these kids wouldn't have been born anyway.

Good luck, Canada.

NET WORTH | NOV. 14, 2006

Sharing anti-malaria medication with Belinda Stronach at the Hotel Rwanda is not the strangest experience of my life, but it's up there.

This was two summers ago, and it was near the end of a trip to Africa where we followed Dr. Jeffrey Sachs, director of the Earth Institute at Columbia University, as he visited Millennium Village sites, gave speeches, met with aid workers and lobbied governments. I won't bother raving about Sachs. Suffice it to say the guy is brilliant. Sachs is considered one of the leading economists in the world, and he is the only academic to have been repeatedly ranked among the world's most influential people by *Time* magazine. Basically I have nothing in common with the man.

The entire trip to Africa with Belinda and Sachs was truly surreal. I don't think an hour went by where I didn't ask myself how in the hell I got there.

Before Africa, I didn't know Belinda at all really. I interviewed her when she was a Tory, and between takes it came up that she was a friend of Dr. Sachs. She talked about how brilliant he was, and of course I agreed. What she didn't know was that the entire time she talked about Dr. Jeffrey Sachs I thought she meant Dr. Oliver Sacks, the guy who specialized in bizarre brain disorders and who was portrayed by Robin Williams in the movie *Awakenings.*

The more Belinda talked about how much she thought of Sachs and how he helped her out as a policy adviser during her leadership campaign, the stranger I thought Belinda was. I remember thinking, "Why would she want a world-renowned expert on Tourette's syndrome to advise her on a leadership run for the Tories?" I knew many Tory MPs at the time were afflicted with the condition, but I still found it extreme.

After the interview ended, Belinda told me she hoped to go to Africa with Sachs someday, and she added, "If it ever comes together I'll give you a call."

It's not the kind of call you actually expect to get—politicians say all sorts of things during small talk.

Later, when I realized what an idiot I'd been, I attempted to remedy the situation by purchasing *The End of Poverty* by Dr. Jeffrey Sachs. It's a very good read, and even though it offers no help for people with brain disorders, I'd recommend it to anyone.

It was over a year later that Belinda called me up out of the blue—she was heading to Africa, and would I like to come? I said yes. I really had no idea what to expect on such a trip, and when I told friends I was going to Africa with Belinda Stronach, they immediately dubbed the trip "Belinda's Pink Champagne Safari." I tend to hang with a cynical bunch.

The trip was put together in record time. I was at the airport before I really found out where we were going. When I saw the list of countries we were visiting, it might as well have been titled

"Places Rick has never wanted to go." Rwanda was on the list. As home of one of the worst genocides in recent history, it was not a destination hot spot in my mind. Ethiopia? Not once in my life had I uttered the phrase, "I'd like to visit Ethiopia someday." The port of Djibouti was on the list, and not being sure where it actually was, I Googled it, and the first entry I came across described the port as "living hell on earth." This was not a Pink Champagne Safari.

I had no idea what to expect, and that was just as well, because nothing would have prepared me. A constant theme of anyone who writes about Africa is the extremes you experience, and my reaction was no different. In Uganda, for example, we spent a day in a village where five thousand people are living in extreme poverty. And even calling it a village doesn't do it justice. The word "village" has a Western connotation that doesn't apply here. Spending a day touring a "village" makes most of us think of a day wasted looking at antique shops and having to suffer the indignity of staying in a bed and breakfast run by batty English people. This wasn't the case here. This "village" had practically no shelter, no water supply, no fuel, near impassable roads, no communications infrastructure, no market and very little in the way of food.

And if one forgot for a second the inequity of the situation, it was driven home by the evening's agenda: visiting the palatial home of the president of Uganda and watching Sachs and the president hammer out a seven-point aid agreement. I'd be lying if I said it wasn't a little hard on the head to spend the day with kids who have never had a real meal in their lives and then spend the evening with some dude who wears a gold hat and has a piano that plays itself.

I swore before I went to Africa that when I came back I wouldn't be transformed into a hemp-wearing dullard armed with a thousand statistics aimed at depressing everyone around me and ruining whatever occasion I happened to be attending. But I did know that it would have some effect on me, and of course it did.

For my entire life I've been pretty good at spotting a problem but not so clever at coming up with the right answers. And if the truth be told, quite often when faced with an overwhelming problem, I'm content to believe that the situation is beyond help, and then it's off to the pub.

This is why getting to know a guy like Dr. Jeffrey Sachs is so dangerous. He's an answer guy, and when you learn the answers and in some cases you see how simple they are, it's hard not to get on board. Which brings me to the "Spread the Net" campaign.

In Africa over a million kids die of malaria every year. That's pretty overwhelming. It was Sachs, however, who told us that it doesn't need to be that way. The answer is simple, tangible, old-fashioned and cost effective. One of the best tools to fight malaria is a mosquito bednet. The net goes over the bed, and usually two or three kids will sleep under the thing. The net is treated with insecticide and will continue to do its job for over five years. If you buy a kid a net, there's a pretty good chance you can save one or two lives. And the cost? Ten bucks.

That's what Spreadthenet.org is all about. If you go to the website, you can give ten bucks and a mosquito bednet will be purchased and distributed for free in the first two targeted countries—Liberia and Rwanda.

Can anyone think of a better way for Canadians to lend a hand? Malaria is spread by mosquitoes. If there is a war that Canadians can get behind, it's the war on mosquitoes. We spend enough of our time coming up with ways to kill them at home; let's spread the love in Africa.

So at the risk of coming across like the dullard armed with statistics, this past week I went to Montreal with Belinda Stronach and together we launched the Spread the Net campaign. Dr. Sachs was there with us, and at the press conference he spoke about malaria and bednets in a way that I never could.

It was a big success. The website is simple and straightforward. Everyone seems to like the idea and its simplicity. One net, ten bucks, save a life. Belinda worked the phones like a maniac, and we were in a position to announce that $300,000 had already been raised. That's a lot of nets.

We all know that Canadians have a huge capacity for helping out others less fortunate, and already lots of people are coming forward with ideas on how individuals, groups, businesses, churches and universities can help spread the net.

The campaign launch was a great result of an unexpected trip. But I have to admit, my favourite moment was as surreal as the trip itself. There was Dr. Sachs, one of the world's leading economists, a man who spends every waking hour trying to understand the big problems of the world—and then providing the answers. He spoke passionately and eloquently about how we can make a difference in Africa. And when it was over and he had finished speaking, there was a pause, and the first question asked was about Ralph Klein and cracks he made about Belinda's sex life.

The look on his face was one of total bewilderment.

Any comment, Dr. Sachs?

For once he didn't have an answer.

www.spreadthenet.org

DIVING WITH ALEXANDRE DESPATIE

The highest platform, Centre Claude-Robillard, Montreal. Broadcast Nov. 21, 2006

DESPATIE: Now we're ready for the big one.

MERCER: OK, so what do you do—plug your nose?

DESPATIE: Preferably not. You might need your arms to balance the fall.

MERCER: Do you cup your gentleman?

DESPATIE: No, he should be good too—if you fall straight.

MERCER: That's what you said down there, and I'm injured.

DESPATIE: OK, so you cup Mr. President.

MERCER: No, *Gail,* please.

DESPATIE: OK—*Gail*. Sorry. You cup *Gail* and then you should be ready to fall in.

THRONE FOR A LOOP

When Stéphane Dion first became leader of the Liberal party I joined the chorus of pundits telling him to tread carefully and not trigger an election out of the gate by voting against the Throne Speech. Seemed to me the man needed some time to get his house in order.

Who could have foreseen how opposed to triggering an election he would become? The leader of the opposition is supposed to oppose, whereas the only thing Dion seems to oppose is opposing.

Eventually he'll have to pull the trigger, but I can't even imagine what it will take to convince him. He seems like a man who not only embraces abstaining but actually gets off on it. I don't know if the man wears a hair shirt under those snappy suits but it wouldn't surprise me.

As far as getting his house in order? He seems like a somewhat confused home handyman who has all the big power tools and just enough confidence to hack away at the place until it eventually falls down around him.

Will he eventually triumph and become prime minister of Canada? Stranger things have happened. I can't think of any examples, but...

DON'T DO IT, DION | OCT. 9, 2007

There's one week to go to the big Throne Speech and if the Liberals vote against it, boom—there is going to be an election. Which for Stéphane Dion could only be described as a kamikaze move.

The problem here is you've got all these Liberals and every time they look at Stephen Harper all they see is a bully. And you know what? He is a bully. That's what he does. Unfortunately for the Liberals, he's really good at it.

I don't know where Stéphane Dion's adviser went to high school, but I'm worried they're buying into this whole "all bullies are cowards" myth. As in, if you stand up to a bully face to face they will drop like a bag of chips. Well, Stéphane, I hate to tell you, brother, but this is not an after-school special, this is a federal election, and sometimes when you stand up to a bully they just punch you in the head even harder. Do yourself a favour, wait a while.

And the irony here is, this isn't even all Stéphane Dion's fault. It's not his fault the Liberal party has no money. It's not his fault that half the people at Liberal party headquarters have the press gallery on speed-dial. No, he's just the poor sucker who won the leadership race. A prize that apparently comes with a few months in a nice house followed by an ass-kicking.

Stéphane, I know you're worried that if you don't stand up to big bad Harper you're going to look like a coward, and it's true, you will. But believe me, there are worse things in life than looking like a coward. Being dead, for example—politically speaking of course. So before the big Throne Speech, look in the mirror and you ask yourself: Am I ready for a fight? Because believe me, Stephen Harper does that every day. And every day the answer is yes.

BACK TO SCHOOL | OCT. 16, 2007

Parliament has finally reopened and all the members are back at school. I'm worried sick about the little darlings. I just hope they got enough rest, because thanks to Stephen Harper proroguing Parliament, they only got 116 days off this summer. That's like 30 days more than your average grade three student. With that much time lying around, I'm surprised most of them don't have bedsores.

But all that aside, today was their big day. And just like in grade three, they showed up with their shiny new school clothes on—except for Stéphane Dion.

Of course, he had his trusty backpack. Now personally, I don't care that the leader of the opposition runs around with an old backpack. What kills me is that he calls it his "lucky" backpack. Of course, luck is subjective.

For Stéphane Dion, after today's Throne Speech, getting hit by a bus might seem lucky.

And then, of course, we have our leader, Prime Minister Harper. One day back and, in case you missed it, he's had enough of this whole minority government thing. He says he doesn't care that only 36 per cent of Canadians voted for him—he's going to proceed like he has an actual majority. Oh, that's really going to work. Imagine if your surgeon said to you, "Oh, by the way, I only passed 36 per cent of my classes but I'm going to proceed like I'm qualified. Now drop your pants and cough."

Somehow I can't help but think that this is going to end badly. Especially seeing that, at this point, it looks like both sides are just trying to figure out a way to blame the other side, go home again and have another election.

Hey, Stephen—here's a novel idea. You got elected to run a country. Why don't you start acting like it, and instead of trying to figure out new ways to close the place down, why don't you do what every other Canadian did well over a month ago and realize summer's over and get back to work?

SPOUSAL BENEFIT | OCT. 23, 2007

How about that Throne Speech? Talk about a build-up.

Usually these things come and go without a peep. But not with this government. Stephen Harper wanted the speech to have the weight of an American State of the Union address and so, for the first time in decades, it aired on the CBC in prime time.

And boy, there was forty minutes that seemed like four hours.

I just felt bad for all those Canadians who tuned in looking for *Just for Laughs* in its regularly scheduled time slot. You can imagine how disappointed they were—they were on the couch after a hard day at work, with their beer open and the chips in the bowl, ready to watch some funny French people scare the hell out of each other, and all they got was some woman in a big throne, sitting next to another guy in a big throne, and she's reading to Stephen Harper out of a storybook.

Now personally, I love the Throne Speech. If for no other reason than it always makes Canadians think, "What the hell do we have a throne for anyway?"

And I know that Canada is a constitutional monarchy, and the minute anyone says anything about getting rid of the governor general the place goes up. But as a nation, can we at least agree to get rid of the spouse?

I mean, it's a little absurd. He does nothing and yet he gets a throne. Meanwhile, the prime minister gets a folding chair, and the head of the Canadian Forces has to stand?

How about we just take his throne, donate it to an amateur theatre company in Flin Flon, and tell the husband if he wants to watch, he can watch on TV like everyone else?

And who really wants to go to work with their spouse

anyway? How many guys out there have said to their wives, "Honey, I know it's a big deal for you, but I'm not going to your office Christmas party. All you do is talk about work, I don't know anyone and all I do is end up sitting there like an idiot, watching your boss stare at your breasts."

Which was basically the Throne Speech in a nutshell. That, and still no mention of a personal income tax cut from so-called Conservatives.

At least with *Just for Laughs*, the laughs are intentional.

IN THE ARMY NOW

In politics you hear the phrase "public service" bandied about a lot. I've certainly seen some pretty impressive displays of public service over the years, but the greatest examples have not been on Canadian soil. They've been in Bosnia, Kabul, Kandahar and the Persian Gulf.

Members of the Canadian Forces have a hard life. Never mind that they often have to risk their lives in the line of duty, but they must do so with a smile and without expressing an opinion.

Politicians of all stripes like nothing more than to use the Forces as a football for partisan ends. In Canada lately Stephen Harper has taken a page from the Republican playbook and is happy to suggest that anyone who disagrees with his policies is somehow against the men and women who wear the uniform of the Canadian Forces. The irony being that the men and women in uniform have absolutely nothing to do with those policies. They simply go to work every day, risking their lives and following the orders of their political masters. In return they get used as pawns at every turn.

My trips overseas have been among the most exciting and personally rewarding experiences of my life. And no matter what the future holds, no matter what political party is in power, I hope they are visits that can continue.

O'CONNOR SHOULD KNOW BETTER | OCT. 7, 2005

Some time in the future I will be visiting with the Canadian Forces in Afghanistan. I agreed, for security reasons, to keep my mouth shut about this. This morning, however, I discovered the Conservatives have no problem talking about the trip and—surprise, surprise—they are outraged.

In the Toronto *Sun,* Conservative defence critic Gordon O'Connor has blasted the Department of Defence for allowing "civilians" into a war zone.

May I suggest that as a former brigadier general, O'Connor should know that wherever there are Canadian troops stationed, there are civilians. Canadian civilians do much of the important support work for our men and women in uniform, including in war zones. And civilians like me, whose skills are woefully limited to strumming a guitar or telling a joke, have been making these trips since World War I.

It's called entertaining the troops. It's not a great sacrifice on the entertainer's part; in fact, it's a great privilege. Showbiz folk love a captive audience and we will gladly travel across the world and visit a war zone to find one.

If Canada as a nation is going to have troops positioned abroad, in harm's way, members of the Canadian Forces and their families have to know that the country stands with them. Mr. O'Connor is not sending that message.

In the *Sun* article, Mr. O'Connor seems to indicate that his real problem with the idea of "high-profile Canadians" going to Afghanistan comes from a desire to protect families. He is quoted as saying, "How are they going to explain to the families if some of these people get hit by bombs when they're over there?"

I would suggest they would explain it in the same way they have had to explain such occurrences in the past. I would also respectfully suggest to Mr. O'Connor that as an adult civilian, I'm allowed to make my own decisions concerning the risks I take in my own personal life. And don't worry—in the event of an accident, the taxpayer will not be on the hook. I have signed my release form.

For the time being, the Tory position is that visits to Afghanistan be limited to "Defence Department officials and politicians who oversee the forces."

I can't speak for business leaders and athletes, but I can speak for entertainers. If Mr. O'Connor ever becomes Canada's minister of defence and he bars civilian entertainers from visiting the troops but encourages politicians to do so, he had better be prepared to put on a pair of heels and a dress and learn to sing for his supper.

WHERE'S MY ARMOUR? | OCT. 19, 2005

I have just returned from a week in Afghanistan. It would be near impossible to sum up the entire experience, but here are a few observations.

There are lots of rules in the Canadian Forces. A very simple rule is that you must have your flak jacket and helmet with you at all times, and when you are not wearing them you must know where they are. This is pretty important. Camp Julian in Kabul was the target of a rocket attack just days before we arrived, as was the Canadian embassy. If you're going to hang out in these places, it makes sense that you know where your armour is.

This does not seem to be a problem for most soldiers; I know this because when you look around the Canadian camps you don't see abandoned flak jackets or helmets. Well actually, last week you might have because I was there, and try as I might to keep track of my things, I kept laying mine down and then inevitably I would see something shiny or get talking to some soldiers who would then lead me elsewhere to meet other soldiers and eventually I would be on the other side of the camp with no idea where I'd left the bloody things.

On one occasion, as I was once again wandering around looking for my helmet, a soldier asked me sarcastically if, in my other job, I have people who follow me around keeping track of my clothing. In fact I do. It's called the Wardrobe Department. I chose not to pass this on, as it seemed a bit unmanly.

The other problem I would have is the briefings. They love to give briefings in the army. A briefing is a bit like school. At least it seemed like school to me, because more often than not I didn't have a bloody clue what anyone was talking about.

Also there is the matter of cowardice. Perhaps I shall write about my overall cowardice in great length at another time.

On the second last day of the trip, Guy Lafleur woke up and played ball hockey with the soldiers first thing in the morning, then put in a full day that ended with a four-hour flight to another camp in a Herc. When we arrived, Guy went and played another full game of hockey, at nine o'clock that night. He signed literally hundreds of autographs every day and seemed to accept that many men serving their country overseas were Leafs fans. I shared a room with Guy on a stopover at an airbase on the way in and out of the country; having to wake up Guy Lafleur at 4:30 in the morning so we could go get on a Herc was one of the most surreal moments of my life. Guy . . . Guy . . . Guy . . . wake up! *Rapide comme une bunny!*

Arseholes are a fact of life but, as God is my witness, I never met any on this trip, and I met about seven hundred people. This must qualify as a statistical anomaly.

This was my second trip to Afghanistan, and the capital city of Kabul has changed dramatically since Canada showed up. Kabul looks and feels like a city on the mend. New construction is everywhere, the stores are crowded, there is fresh produce in abundance and women are seen everywhere on the streets—many without burkas.

Canada has played a huge part in this transformation. Now things start to get real tricky. The bulk of Canada's troops will soon be stationed in Kandahar. This is the Wild West. Kandahar is, bottom line, far more dangerous than Kabul. Inside the front gates of the Canadian camp sits a British armoured vehicle that was recently hit by a suicide bomber. Because of the armour, everyone walked away from that attack. Canadians on patrol in this area now drive similar vehicles, made by Mercedes.

In Kandahar we were lucky enough to go along on a foot patrol. The kids go crazy for the Canadian soldiers and mob them wherever they go. They want high fives and pens.

CHRISTMAS IN FLAK JACKETS | DEC. 28, 2006

A few months ago General Rick Hillier promised me a Christmas I would never forget; turns out he is a man of his word.

This year, on Christmas morning, I was in Sperwan Ghar in the Panjwai district of Afghanistan sitting around a single-burner Coleman stove with a dozen Canadian soldiers. Rush was on the stereo, and we were watching a pot of Tetley tea bags threaten to boil. Outside it was wet and muddy, but inside the sandbag bunker where these Royal Canadian Dragoons ate and slept, it was warm and as comfortable as one could expect under the circumstances. Corporal Frank Farrell was in charge of the pot, and there was no top on it this morning—this was not to be rushed.

General Hillier is a very persuasive man. He is also a Newfoundlander. And while he is the chief of the Canadian Forces, it has been suggested that he might think he is the chief of all Newfoundlanders. He'll call you up and suggest to you that on December 25 there is only one place you should be and it's so special that by agreeing to go there you render your life insurance null and void. You aren't asked so much as you are voluntold.

This was my third trip to Afghanistan, but my first at Christmas. General Hillier was on a personal mission to shake hands with every man and woman wearing a Canadian uniform in Afghanistan and the Persian Gulf, and I was along for the ride. The way he described it was simple: "It's Christmas," he said, "and all we are going to do is pop in and say hello to a few folks." In Canada "popping in to say hello" at Christmas is just a matter of arranging for a designated driver or making sure you have cab fare in your pocket. This was a little more complicated. It started with a nine-hour flight overseas, stopping in Croatia for gas, and then onward to a military base that dare not speak its name or reveal its location. Once there we immediately boarded a Sea King helicopter for a night flight across the water so we could land on the deck of the HMCS *Ottawa*.

On this leg of the trip there were three other Newfoundlanders—broadcaster Max Keeping, singer-songwriter Damhnait Doyle and my old colleague Mary Walsh—and three members of the Conservative caucus—whip Jay Hill, MP Laurie Hawn and President of the Treasury Board John Baird. I was happy they were issued flak jackets and helmets because I had a sneaking suspicion that the combination of Walsh and the three Tories might make some recent skirmishes with the Taliban insurgency seem tame in comparison. If it came down to a three-on-one donnybrook, my money was on the Princess Warrior.

And so, on the night before Christmas Eve, our little gang of Newfoundlanders, along with fifty or so sailors, closed the mess on the HMCS *Ottawa*. We laughed until we were stupid. It felt like Christmas.

After sunrise General Hillier addressed the troops on the deck of the ship. This was the first of countless speeches he would give over the next four days. He is funny as hell and as inspiring as anyone I have ever seen speak. He makes soldiers laugh and then he makes them cry. He thanks them all in a way that makes everyone grow inches. From a show-business perspective he is a tough act to follow, but follow we did. When it came Damhnait's turn to say a few words, she sang a song, and if there is a better way to kick off an adventure than watching Damhnait Doyle and 250 sailors sing *O Canada* on the deck of a Canadian battleship as it sails the Gulf, I can't think of it.

After the *Ottawa* it was straight back to the base for a three-hour nap before a 3 a.m. wake-up call for the flight to Kandahar. Once in Kandahar, we had the standard briefing that is mandatory for visiting entertainers and/or the head-injured. When the siren goes, do what you're told; when everything seems fine, do what you're told; and when in doubt, do what you're told.

From there we went "over the wire." It was Christmas Eve, and General Hillier wanted to make it to all the forward operating bases. These bases are all former Taliban strongholds. For the most part they are high points of land that were hard fought for. Some of the bases are nothing but points of land with soldiers living in tents, trenches and bunkers. This is the front line of a war.

Charlie Company at Patrol Base Wilson was the first group we spoke to. These are the men and women who are working under maximum threat levels in Afghanistan. They are out there on patrol every day, for days at a time, engaging the enemy. They have all lost friends here. They have a bit of the ten-thousand-mile stare—which is to be expected—so from the point of view of a guy who stands around and tells jokes for a living, this is what you would call a tough crowd. General Hillier was right, though. He told me that just showing up was enough and anything else was a bonus.

That afternoon we made our way by convoy to Strong Point West, home to Bravo Company. This was still Christmas Eve, and we arrived in time to help serve their Christmas meal. General Hillier worked the turkey, senior officers worked the potatoes and vegetables, and I pulled up the rear as chief gravy server. I must admit I felt pretty darn important serving the gravy. These guys get a cooked meal about every three to four days. For the most part they eat rations out of a bag wherever they find themselves. Plus they get shot at. Anything hot with gravy is a very, very big deal. As the man with the gravy ladle I was probably—for the duration of the serving line—the most popular man on Earth.

And so this year for Christmas dinner I sat on the ground in the dust and ate turkey loaf and gravy on a paper plate. Everyone except me had a gun. There was lots of talk of home, and like at anyone's Christmas dinner there were lots of pictures. At one point the designated photographers had ten digital cameras in their hands at a time trying to get the group shots.

Everywhere you go in Afghanistan where there are Canadian soldiers, you see Christmas cards and letters supporting the troops. Some of the tents and accommodations are decorated with so many homemade cards from school kids that you would swear you had wandered into an elementary-school lunchroom and not a mess hall. It's amazing to see groups of battle-weary soldiers wrapped in ammunition and guns stopping to read these things with the attention that is usually reserved solely for the parent. I was in a tent with two guys in their early twenties who were poring over a stack of letters and class photos and separating them into piles. I was a little taken aback that these young guys, in the middle of a war zone, would be so moved by support from grade-four classes until I realized the deciding factor for the favourites pile was which teacher was hotter.

On Christmas morning, the convoy headed to Sperwan Ghar. The troops here sleep in dugouts with sandbag perimeters. After the speeches and hellos, a corporal asked me back to his quarters for a cup of tea. He was, like so many guys here, a Newfoundlander. And so that's where I spent Christmas morning, watching corporal Frank Farrell stir the teapot while a dozen or so guys hung out and exchanged cards and had a few laughs. The crowd in the bunker wasn't there just for the tea. They had been waiting a long time for Corporal Farrell to open the Eversweet margarine tub that he had received a few weeks earlier in the mail. In the tub was his mom's Christmas cake. When the tea was perfect and our paper cups were filled, the tape was pulled from the tub and we all agreed: Bernadette Farrell makes the best Christmas cake in Canada.

The trip carried on. We visited more forward operating bases. General Hillier made good on his goal of shaking hands with practically every soldier in harm's way this Christmas. And by late afternoon we took the convoy back through "ambush ally" to the main base in Kandahar for the prime show of the tour, for about eight hundred soldiers in the newly opened Canada House.

Max Keeping was our master of ceremonies, General Hillier gave a speech of a lifetime, Mary Walsh made me laugh like the old days, Damhnait Doyle sang like an angel and the Montreal rock band Jonas played late into the night. I was supposed to take the mic for fifteen minutes, but I stayed for twenty-five. A tad selfish, but honestly I can't imagine I will have so much fun performing ever again.

Everywhere we went on this trip, men and women in uniform thanked our little gang for giving up our Christmas to be with them in Afghanistan. I know that I speak for everyone when I say we gave very little and we received far too much. We met great friends, we had lots of laughs and dare I say had the best Christmas ever.

MR. DION GOES TO WAR | JAN. 22, 2008

Afghanistan is becoming a popular travel destination—especially if you're a politician. In fact, for two years in a row now, it's beating Florida.

Basically, every member of Parliament in this country wants to go. This is retail politics 101. You get off the plane, you put on the helmet, you make sure it's not on backwards, you get your picture taken with a couple of soldiers and a few Afghani youngsters, you come home, you get a bump in the polls. It's almost impossible to screw up. It's why it's one of the few things that Stephen Harper allows his cabinet ministers to do without adult supervision.

It's also why Stéphane Dion has been asking to go for a very long time. And this past week, the Tories finally said yes. So off Dion went. And boy did he make a balls of it.

The man comes back from Afghanistan, and he says Canada should pull out of combat by 2009. Fine, that's always been his position. But then he throws in, as an afterthought, that perhaps NATO should consider invading Pakistan. Wow, I never saw that one coming. You know, it's not every day that a Canadian politician suggests invading another country, especially a country with the bomb.

The Tories, of course, loved this, but while Dion might have put his foot in his mouth, what the Tories did was far worse. When politicians visit Afghanistan, it's always a secret. Those are the rules, written by the military. The military are very, very touchy about this. They don't want the Taliban to know when politicians are visiting because then they become a target. And shag the politicians; remember, it's the soldiers who are guarding the politicians you have to worry about.

So Dion, true to his word, never told a soul he was going. His staff didn't even know he was going. But the

Tories, they said, "The hell with the military," and they had a cabinet minister, Helena Guergis, release details of the visit. Sure, Canadian military lives were put at risk, but I guess that's the price you have to pay when you're facing re-election in Simcoe-Grey.

Now, I don't know why the Tories did this. I mean, if Michael Ignatieff or Bob Rae called the Taliban and told them that Dion was coming, that would make sense. But this is just Tories being Tories. It's like they can't even stop themselves.

Now it's over, I'm glad Dion made the trip, if for no other reason it shows us one more thing that the Liberals and Tories have in common: they both say they support our troops, but what they really love is using them.

ON A ROLL WITH PIERRE BERTON

Broadcast Feb. 21, 2005

PIERRE BERTON: And remember, Canada, it's the loose joints that tend to fall apart, leaving unsightly toke burns on your chairs or on your bow tie.

OUR NEIGHBOURS TO THE SOUTH

Ah yes—there's a lot more to this relationship than softwood, you know.

ALL ABOUT THE OIL | JAN. 12, 2004

France, Russia, Germany and Canada have been excluded from bidding on Iraqi reconstruction contracts. Prime Minister Martin says this is unfair.

Paul, this seems whiny to me. I mean, we were against the war, we said America was just going over there to steal oil and now we're like . . . *Hey! How come we don't get some of the stolen oil?* We're cool with getting a little bit of the back end. We're like a guy who sat out a bank robbery and then wants a cut. "Come on, I was the, uh, backup getaway driver."

LET'S BE NICE TO THEM | JAN. 19, 2004

When it comes to this American Missile Defence Shield, our friends and neighbours to the south have been very consistent. They've said time and again they would appreciate Canada's help but they don't need Canada's help and they don't care what we have to say on the subject because quite frankly they're going to build the thing anyway. Which is exactly what you'd expect. But lately some experts in America are saying that in order to make this shield work, they're going to need a few fancy-shmancy satellite-tracking stations in the North, which, lo and behold, belongs to Canada.

This must be driving Donald Rumsfeld completely nuts. Suddenly the only thing standing between him and his Buck Rogers missile shield is a nation of pot-smoking, homo-loving peaceniks. And sure, they know that Chrétien's gone and they know that's a good thing. But they don't know Paul Martin from a hole in the ground.

The only thing they really know about Paul Martin is what they learned on a Google search. The man's good with money and apparently he once ate an entire pan of hash brownies. They also know that no Canadian prime minister ever got in trouble at home for saying no to the Americans.

And Paul Martin's getting a lot of pressure on this missile shield. Jack Layton and the NDP are hysterical; they're saying that this is militarizing space and not making the world a safer place. And it's good to see Jack Layton and the NDP hysterical because . . . well, because that's their job. But it doesn't change the fact that if the Americans want to build an American missile shield, that's their business. And if they want to put a few tracking stations in Canada, what are we supposed to say? "Ummm, sorry, but we looked and, ummm, we just don't have the room."

I say that as long as this doesn't cost us any money, and they put in their own road, their own hydro, and they don't piss off the Inuit, they can go up north and they can track satellites until their heads fall off. And Jack, that's not sucking up to America; that's just being nice to the neighbours.

GO INVADE YOURSELF | FEB. 6, 2004

Just looking at George Bush you can tell he's as mad as hell. He can't believe that after all this time there are still no weapons of mass destruction. And I think he's actually surprised. Things were looking good there a couple of weeks ago when they found a can of Raid and a Bic lighter, but since then, nothing.

Which is why Bush has announced the formation of a special investigation into weapons of mass destruction. Basically he wants to know just what the hell he's been up to for the past year and a half. He's saying, I don't trust me, I'm going to get to the bottom of this, I'm either with me or against me. So he's going to spend a fortune figuring out just how intelligent U.S. intelligence really is.

Boy, it's a shame to see someone waste their money, isn't it? I could just go knock on the door of the embassy and tell them what the rest of us already know. But no. He wants to know why it is that when he said there were weapons of mass destruction everyone knew he was lying except him.

And you know why he didn't know, don't you? Dick Cheney forgot to tell him. I just hope he doesn't take the news too hard; otherwise he might have no choice but to go invade himself. And no getting around it, that's going to hurt.

HOW THEY HAVE CANADA BEAT | FEB. 5, 2008

It's Super Tuesday—the most important day in the U.S. primaries as both political parties try to figure out who they're going try to send to the White House. And I'm loving it—despite the fact that I have no idea how it works.

I know, it's democracy in action—but to me, it might as well be Chinese algebra. And yes, I admit, it bugs the hell out of me that the Americans have this system of choosing a leader that according to CNN everyone understands—and I just don't get. I'm much more comfortable assuming *they're* the stunned ones.

But I do know this. From a show business perspective they've got us beat. For starters, they know how to spend the big money. Rudy Giuliani spent 50 million dollars getting his ass kicked just in the state of Florida. That's twice as much money as any Canadian party is going to spend in the next federal election.

And it's not just the big money that makes it exciting. They work these candidates into the ground. They're exhausted. Cripes, there's a national debate on CNN every three hours. Half the fun is flicking on Lou Dobbs every evening to see the bags under Hillary Clinton's eyes get bigger.

And speaking of Hillary, when it comes to casting, we can't touch the U.S. We Canadians think of ourselves as part of this progressive, diverse nation and yet who's running for the top job in big, bad, backwards America? A woman, a black man, a Libertarian, a Mormon with big hair, and some dude who was in a bamboo cage in Vietnam for five and a half years. Meanwhile in Canada, we're gearing up for yet another race between a pudgy white guy and a skinny white guy and some other white guy.

Which may go a long way to explain the other big difference between Canadian and U.S. politics these days: in America, in this race, young people are engaged. In Canada—they're choosing none of the above.

CANADA'S NEARLY NEW GOVERNMENT

When Stephen Harper became prime minister he insisted his lot be called "Canada's new government." Internal party memos revealed he hoped the phrase would be in use until March 2021.

But it soon became clear that most Canadians found this "new government" business a tad ridiculous, an insult to their intelligence. It quickly got old. As a result, the Conservative party has started testing new slogans such as "Now with lemon" and "Contains more fibre."

STEPHEN! STEPHEN! STEPHEN! | JUNE 23, 2005

Confidential

To: Conservative Party of Canada Caucus Members

Re: Opposition Leader's Schedule

Please be advised that Stephen Harper will not be available for regularly scheduled beratings this coming Friday. Leader's schedule has been changed to devote time to the spontaneous charm offensive.

Caucus members are encouraged to memorize leader's schedule, attend events and cheer the leader on in an appropriate manner.

SCHEDULE FOR FRIDAY

5:00 p.m. Leader to spontaneously bump into Rona Ambrose and Conservative youth caucus by Centennial flame.

5:05 p.m. Leader will refer to Rona and youth caucus as the "hottie and her peeps."

Assembled caucus and observers are encouraged to raise right hand, form a fist, make a circular motion and chant "Stephen! Stephen! Stephen!"

CTV *Countdown with Mike Duffy* crew to be in attendance.

5:10 p.m. Leader and youth caucus to travel on foot to Byward Market, where leader will spontaneously announce he is getting nipple pierced.

Canadian Press photographer to attend.

Photo of leader's nipple being iced to be released immediately.

5:30 p.m. Leader to sit on deck at Milestones restaurant located near the Château Laurier. Leader will order and enjoy a domestic beer. Members of caucus are invited to stop by and "Have a cold one with Stephen."

While seated, leader will roll up shirt sleeves and expose yellow Lance Armstrong cancer bracelet. Jane Taber to be informed that "Stephen relaxed and ordered a domestic beer just like a regular guy, he talked about hockey and declared, 'Anyone who drinks imported is a pansy.'"

(Note to caucus: Many of you have voiced your concerns over our last memo, encouraging you to wear the yellow cancer bracelet. We have looked into your concerns and have determined that the yellow cancer bracelet does not cause cancer but is part of a campaign to beat cancer.)

6:45 p.m. Secret Hacky Sack lessons (closed to media).

CONSERVATIVE CABINET REVEALED | JAN. 9, 2006

Many sports fans spend their days building fantasy football or baseball teams. Likewise there is a handful of nerds out there who create fantasy cabinets. I do this all the time. I often kill time at the airport compiling my dream cabinet in the back of a scribbler. This week, for example, my dream cabinet would contain John Crosbie, Geddy Lee and Justin Pogge. Luckily for the nation I will never choose a cabinet so we will never know what kind of damage I could wreak on the country.

I have it on very good authority, however, that Stephen Harper is spending a lot of time playing the game these days. Word is the back room on the Harper bus resembles the woodshed from *A Beautiful Mind:* the walls are littered with the names of potential Conservative cabinet ministers. Luckily, my secret mole in the Tory campaign (Tom Flanagan) has been forwarding me photos of the notes with his hand-held Palm device. This is what the Tory cabinet looks like so far.

Stockwell Day (Okanagan-Coquihalla)—Minister of Foreign Affairs

Stockwell Day is perhaps the most experienced and most talented member on the Conservative front bench. Stockwell is currently foreign affairs critic for the Conservative party and he has done a bang-up job. When he was questioned as to why his party did not offer condolences to the Palestinians on the death of Yasser Arafat, Stock responded by sending out a column by David Frum that speculated Yasser had died of AIDS.

With Stock representing Canada on the world stage, can peace in the Middle East be far away?

Jason Kenney (Calgary Southeast)—Minister of Health

Jason Kenney is an embarrassment of riches for the Conservative party. He is one of Stephen Harper's most trusted lieutenants and is experienced, well liked and hirsute. He is perfectly suited to a mélange of cabinet positions, and while he has a grasp on all the issues, health seems to be his forte.

> "I do support the idea of private health care."
> —Jason Kenney, Conservative Party critic
> on Canada-U.S. Relations, October 31, 2000

Rob Anders (Calgary West)—Minister of State (Multiculturalism)

Rob Anders is the man to reach out to Canada's diverse multicultural communities.

> "Nelson Mandela is a terrorist."
> —Rob Anders

> "Rob is a true reformer and a true conservative. He has been a faithful supporter of mine and I am grateful for his work."
>
> —Stephen Harper, endorsing Rob Anders

Vic Toews (Provencher)—Minister of Justice

Vic is the current justice critic, and he takes the bull by the horns. He believes the notwithstanding clause should be used to override minority rights. He calls it the "ultimate tool," and so it is. The notwithstanding clause can be used to take away the rights of gay people to marry each other or the rights of the Chinese to drive. If you're white and straight, the chance of this being used against you are slim to none. This is for uppity minorities only. In case of emergency uppity-ness, please break glass.

Art Hanger (Calgary Northeast)—Minister of Citizenship and Immigration

> "Immigrants are choking welfare systems, contributing to high unemployment, and many cannot read."
>
> —Conservative MP Art Hanger

Myron Thompson (Wild Rose)—Minister of State (Youth Justice)

"Let's lower the age to ten."

—MP Myron Thompson,
commenting on the age at which he
believes one should be tried as an
adult, at a Vernon, BC, meeting

David Sweet—Minister Responsible for the Status of Women

"There's a particular reason why Jesus called men only. It's not that women aren't co-participators. It's because Jesus knew women would naturally follow. Men, on the other hand, had to be called."

—Conservative candidate David Sweet,
former president and
CEO of Promise Keepers Canada

Brian Fitzpatrick—Minister of Indian Affairs and Northern Development

"You can't scalp me because I haven't got much hair on top of my head."

—Conservative candidate Brian Fitzpatrick

Darrel Reid—Minister Responsible for the Canadian Wheat Board

"I think every Christian's under an obligation to change laws to reflect biblical values. Different Christians are going to try to change different laws, according to the call God gives them. You see Christians in all political parties. That reflects different understandings of what God's call is to us. That's a healthy thing. If the yeast congregates in one part of the loaf, it makes for pretty bad bread."

—Conservative candidate Darrel Reid,
former president of Focus on the
Family Canada

Cheryl Gallant (Renfrew-Nipissing-Pembroke)—Women's Caucus Chair

"We saw that young American having his head cut off. What's happening, what is happening down there is no different."

—Cheryl Gallant
at a 2004 pro-life rally on Parliament Hill,
comparing abortion to the beheading of
American Nicolas Berg by insurgents in Iraq

Of course, this is just a fraction of what the final cabinet will look like. Harper will have to come up with another twenty-five cabinet ministers. There is a rumour, however, that he might make history and appoint himself minister of everything, removing all MPs from the process.

ALL HIS FAULT | JAN. 31, 2006

This is a very exciting time for anyone who views politics as a blood sport in Canada. After all, it's not every day that we go out and choose a new prime minister. And when we do, there's a certain similarity to them. But only in the sense that they're usually Liberal lawyers from Quebec. Anything else is a breath of fresh air, and that is what Stephen Harper is.

The man is a breath of fresh air with just a hint of Head and Shoulders. Confidence in him is high, and so it should be. All across this great country—except, of course P.E.I.—Canadians went into the polling booth and they said, I'm going stand up for Canada and make Harper my fearless leader. Of course, it's too soon to say how he's going to do, but I will say this—that man looks damn fine in a turtleneck, and if he can do as good a job running this country as he did running a campaign, we're going to be laughing.

He ran one hell of a campaign. Although to be fair, he had some good luck. Now, I'm not saying it was all good luck, or that his luck is going to change or even that his luck has gone away forever. All I'm saying is the campaign is over, he's been elected for only eight days and already Ford has laid off thirty-five hundred people, mad cow is suddenly back and Mario Lemieux has left the world of hockey forever. Who are we going to blame? Stephen Harper and his anti-job, pro-mad-cow, anti-hockey agenda.

Now hopefully, this bit of bad luck won't continue when he names his cabinet. I'm not concerned. I believe there are plenty of competent Conservative MPs out there. In fact, I can think of ten Tories off the top of my head who would make excellent cabinet ministers. The problem is, of course, you need twenty-five if you want to make a cabinet. Yes, it's going to be an interesting four years, Mr. Harper. Or three years or two years or even one. Time will tell. But I will say this: welcome to the show, Prime Minister. From here on in, no matter what happens, it's all your fault.

THE DISCIPLINARIAN | MAR. 28, 2006

When Stephen Harper first got elected, he made it pretty clear that he's the kind of guy that gets off on discipline. Hey, fine by me. But lately I'm starting to think that here's a man who might get turned on by discipline just a little bit too much.

According to Harper's new rules, members of his cabinet aren't allowed to write a letter to the editor without his permission. Think about that. We live in a country where a ten-year-old girl can write a letter to the paper about a local issue but not your conservative MP. Harper's basically saying, "Oh, my health minister can be trusted with the welfare of 35 million people but not with a pen and paper. He's too flaky."

And no speaking in public, either. When Harper went to Afghanistan, he was accompanied by the defence minister, but Harper didn't introduce him to the troops once. Think about that. We live in a country where the defence minister can't address soldiers because he might say something stupid. And now the latest changes. The media has been banned from standing outside the cabinet room. For over thirty years, when cabinet ministers left that room they had to walk past reporters. But not anymore. Harper's banned the media, put them downstairs so his ministers can now skulk out the back without ever being seen.

I swear to you this man is doing everything in his power to ensure that later on these people can't get picked in a lineup. I don't know what Harper's plan is, but I know this. If you're the prime minister and the first thing you do is ban the media and then devise an escape route, don't be surprised if people think you're up to no good.

DADDY MADE A BOO-BOO | MAY 25, 2007

At this moment, in an undisclosed location, the Tory brain trust is huddled in a room desperately trying to figure out a way to get the Conservatives' polling numbers up. Oh to be a fly on the wall—a wall that is no doubt dripping in blood.

For a while it was looking good for the Conservatives. They delivered the biggest-spending budget in Canadian history, they mailed hundreds of millions of dollars to Quebec and they placated the masses with some sort of rebate on the cost of enrolling your kid in hockey. Sure, their base was alienated by a budget that refused regular working Canadians a personal income tax cut, but a decision had been made that the base could suffer. In fact, no Canadian government has so readily abandoned its base and with such confidence.

And for a shining moment the big spending seemed to pay off. The polls showed they were up, way up in fact, passing the magic number that would guarantee a majority. And then in a stunning move the master chess player who is the prime minister, the man who admits he thinks about political strategy twenty-four hours a day, blinked. He looked at the big numbers and decided he had nowhere to go but up. Oops. Daddy made a boo-boo.

Which brings us back to that increasingly desperate room that houses the brain trust.

No doubt it was there that the recent trip to Afghanistan was hatched. Sending the prime minister into a war zone was actually a very good idea. And thanks to Jim Flaherty's budget, much safer than, say, a trip to Newfoundland, Nova Scotia, Saskatchewan or Bay Street.

It's bold ideas like this that might provide some much-desired momentum, although it's my guess that nobody in the room has the balls to stand up and say, "If we want Canadians to like us more maybe we should stop talking and acting like pricks."

Because really it seems like they just can't help themselves.

Harper's trip to Afghanistan is a perfect example. Given the goodwill that the average Canadian feels toward the soldiers on the ground in Afghanistan, it would take hard work on someone's part to screw up a visit like that.

And yet the Conservatives did.

Members of the media were of course alerted in advance so they could take photos of it happening. When a prime minister, cabinet minister or the chief of defence staff heads into a war zone, journalists are often told in advance. And because it's a war zone they are properly sworn to secrecy. The Harper government upped the ante this time and reporters were not only sworn to secrecy but also told that if they breathed a word about the trip in advance they would and could be arrested and thrown in the clink.

This pretty much sums up the angry-dad government. There is not a reporter alive on the Hill who can remember ever being threatened with jail over a trip like this. Nor is there a reporter who can remember any legitimate news organization reporting the details of a trip like this in advance. That fact is lost on the Harper government.

Despite the rocky start, most of what occurred overseas seemed to work in the prime minister's favour. For one thing, he's to be commended for taking his minister of defence with him again. It's apparently part of a new "bring your cabinet minister to work" program he's testing in response to criticism that he keeps his ministers on a short leash. He interpreted the criticism to mean he was being too easy on his ministers and issued shorter leashes with electric-shock collars, designed to curb barking in house pets. These collars, which are triggered by vibrations of the vocal chords, have had mixed results, however.

John Baird, for example, has taken to wearing the device in an unprescribed manner. As a result he seems to enjoy the sound of his own voice more than he did six months ago (if such a thing is possible). Insiders attribute this to the pulsating shock that is administered to an unknown part of his nether regions whenever he starts barking.

As proof, you only had to watch the twitches of pleasure as he gleefully reported a government employee had been marched out of the Department of the Environment offices in handcuffs for the crime of leaking his climate change plan to someone who apparently cared.

The employee in question, of course, turns out to be a kid on a temporary contract tasked with monitoring the media for mentions of the minister's name. He was, to put it mildly, the lowest man on a very tall totem poll. Not only that, he is also a drummer in a band. What I want to know is—what kind of person lets the drummer have access to a top-secret plan in the first place? Had the minister not met a drummer before?

Baird, rightly so, has no time for this type of so-called "political action." Political action is no excuse for breaking the law. Although Baird did use the same excuse after being dragged away by police for disturbing the peace at Liberal MP Peter Milliken's nomination meeting a few years back.

Perhaps that's why Baird is so angry at this whippersnapper. Perhaps when the minister closes his eyes at night he sees a little bit of himself in the young anarchist. And speaking of anarchists, the brain trust must deal with the fact that the hottest new read on Parliament Hill is the Conservatives' own guide to disrupting Parliament, another document leaked to the *National Post*'s Don Martin.

The 200-page manual, prepared by the PMO, instructs committee chairs on ways to make parliamentary committees hopelessly inefficient to the point that they cease to function. The intention is to sabotage the working of Parliament and then blame the Liberals and the NDP, in order to convince the voters that a minority government can't work.

The idea that such a strategy exists is hardly surprising. The fact they put it in writing takes stupid to a whole new level.

On the upside, the party doesn't seem the least bit upset that this document has been leaked. They are confident that Canadians are simply too stupid to understand the ramifications of a government intentionally causing chaos and deadlock.

So while it is too early to tell if Harper will get a bounce in the polls once the country has seen him stare through binoculars at an Afghani outpost, the hard work continues. Based on past performances I think it's a safe bet to say the Tory brain trust never sleeps. I'm also guessing they are low on blood sugar, but that's purely speculation on my part.

All I do know is that every possible scenario on how to ingratiate Harper into the hearts and minds of Canadians is being suggested in that room.

If only the walls could talk.

They can't of course. If they could, they would have been arrested long ago.

FROM THE DESK OF PRIME MINISTER HARPER | JUNE 1, 2007

Dear Friends and Supporters,

Canada's new government is now sixteen months old.

As for any happy, healthy sixteen-month-old, our every day is full of challenges. One minute things are looking rosy and we seem to have complete control of our faculties, the next minute we become completely irrational, bash our heads against the wall and wet ourselves.

However, we have accomplished much in those sixteen months. Before Canada's new government came to power, parents whose children were enrolled in hockey didn't receive a tax deduction. Canada's new government heard the cry and we answered the call. If your kid is in hockey you can now deduct a dollar thirty a day from your income tax. If you don't have a kid in hockey you are probably gay or lesbian.

Promise made, promise kept, my friends.

Other highlights of the mandate so far? I have seen many hockey games. I met Russian hockey star Vladislav Tretiak and I acquired the services of a personal stylist whose job it is to pick out a lip gloss for me every day. Understand that when I say "I" acquired the services of a stylist what I really mean is that you the taxpayer did. She is on your dime so in many ways that she is Canada's personal stylist, in much the same way the governor general is Canada's governor general.

Also I am proud to say that very early in my mandate I ensured that senior citizens in every province and territory lost billions of dollars they had invested in income trusts. I should add that the hockey games were very exciting for me personally and that I prefer a bubblegum-flavoured gloss over cherry.

Speaking of gloss, I now believe the time has now come for the Conservative Party of Canada to reveal five new priorities. They are:

1. Aboriginal Issues—Canada's new government recognizes that Canada's aboriginal peoples have legitimate land claims that should be dealt with in a timely manner. To this end we promise that we will increase the number of attack ads featuring Stéphane Dion by 50 per cent in the next three months. In the words of great Canadian actor Joe Two Rivers, me like-um Stephen Harper.

2. The Environment—This was always a priority of Canada's new government, but unfortunately a government employee, a bureaucrat, accidentally spilled White-Out on our platform and as a result the word "environment" was lost. This bureaucrat is an incompetent. This was not our fault, this was Public Services' fault. We care about the environment so much we fired a slew of people in the Department of the Environment and are running a new Stéphane Dion attack during the season finale of *Canada's Next Top Model.*

3. Northern sovereignty—The future is in Canada's North. In an effort to ensure that resources in Northern Canada are developed in a responsible way, Canada's new government has instructed the Department of Finance to audit Julie Van Dusen's and Mike Duffy's tax returns for the last eleven years. The Mike Duffys of this world will not stop progress in the North. This must and will stop.

4. Open and Accountable Government. Yes, the catchphrase "open and accountable" will not go away. We are prepared to use it every day and every night. To ensure an even more open government, Communications Director Sandra Buckler will now assume her new position as head of the

RCMP and Canada's spy agency CSIS. We will also cut funding to more museums.

5. This fifth priority is a secret. Any suggestion that we couldn't come up with a fifth priority is scurrilous and unfounded. Any individual, group, media outlet, political party or church group who suggests we have run out of ideas supports the Taliban.

And now if I may, I would like to address one particularly worrisome issue facing Canada. Some of you have written to me stating your concern that the party has strayed from its core principles. As you may have noticed, I did not respond. Please do not take this personally. I simply do not respond to letters. Heck, the parents of a deceased soldier wrote me a letter and I didn't bother responding to them so why would I respond to you? What are you going to do, vote Liberal? Stéphane Dion is not a leader, I am a leader, I am the prime minister of Canada and I don't answer letters unless they pertain to hockey.

Now let me pass on a little anecdote. Yesterday a young man said to me, "Mr. Harper, you are great, thank you for the one-cent GST cut, you are great, see you at Tim Horton's!" This is clearly a great Canadian. I tell that story all the time during family time, which happens at the family table where my family and I gather to enjoy time together as a family.

My friends, I only wish Stéphane Dion understood the importance of family. But he only has one child and she doesn't even live with him. She goes to university in Quebec. I wouldn't be surprised if she ends up studying in France, even. I'm sure he doesn't mind. Liberals hate families more than they hate our troops.

In conclusion let me say God bless Canada and that many Liberals such as Navdeep Baines wear turbans and therefore may or may not be associated with extreme elements.

Yours truly,
Stephen Harper

LACK-OF-PERSONALITY CULT | NOV. 6, 2007

Another National Press Gallery dinner came and went in Ottawa last week.

This is an annual shindig where politicians and members of the media sit down together, have a few beers and eat some rubber chicken, and political leaders of the day make a few silly speeches at their own expense. In 1925 Mackenzie King danced on a table. In 1957 Diefenbaker threw buns at the reporters.

But Stephen Harper's in charge now, and he refused to go. Now this is a very telling decision.

Prime ministers never want to go to this thing, but traditionally they suck it back and go anyway. Politics is a little like junior high. Every year the principal of the school, whether he wants to or not, has to go to the talent show, put on the stupid Hawaiian shirt and the Ray-Bans, and lip-sync to the Spice Girls so that for one shining moment the kids don't think he's a giant tool.

Harper doesn't get this. So he doesn't go. Fine. It's a free country, he can do what he wants. But that's not good enough for him. He has to go one step further and try to ruin it for everyone else by ordering his cabinet ministers to cancel on their dates at the last minute. The truly disturbing thing is, they did.

A lot of us have demanding bosses, but is there a man or woman in Canada with a shred of dignity who would allow their boss to tell them what social events they're allowed to attend on a Saturday night?

Harper's moving out of domineering boss territory and into David Koresh-land. At this point the only things he's missing are the robes and the eleven wives. Just not liking people is now a badge of honour for him.

If I were the Tories I'd be a little bit worried. The economy is red hot, the dollar's through the roof, the GST is coming down, everyone's working and the Tories are still only four points ahead of Stéphane Dion—and everyone thinks he's an idiot.

It is quite possible that despite all the good news the majority of Canadians are never going to sign on to Harper's vision of Canada: where fun is frowned upon but frowning upon others is fun.

THE INVISIBLE GOVERNMENT | JAN. 29, 2008

This week saw the publication of Manley Report, or as it's formally known, "The Independent Panel on Canada's Future Role in Afghanistan." It's a scintillating read. I don't want to give away the ending, but basically it says that Canada should stay the course. It also says that Canadians have no idea what that course is.

For Stephen Harper, the Manley Report is the feel-good read of the year. Because even though his government hasn't bothered to do its job and tell us why we're in Afghanistan, he does not view this as a failure to communicate. He views this as a triumph of modern leadership.

The words "Harper government" and "communicate" have never appeared in the same sentence without the word "won't" in the middle. At first this was a bit of breath of fresh air coming off the Liberals, where you couldn't turn on the TV without seeing some cabinet minister on there blathering on about whatever their department was up to.

But with Harper, the pendulum has swung the other way. He doesn't have cabinet ministers so much as he has chalk outlines on the sidewalk. And to be successful in Harper's cabinet you have to abide by the three D's: don't see, don't hear, don't say. If Helen Keller were alive today, she could have any job she wanted. They promised accountability; they've delivered invisibility.

You could take a hundred bucks, stand on any street corner in Canada and offer people five bucks if they can name three cabinet ministers off the top of their head—double their money if they can name the minister of health. At the end of the day you'd still have enough money for dinner and a movie. Which is exactly the way Stephen Harper likes it. As far as he's concerned, good government is out of sight and out of mind. And fine, that might make his life easier, but he's got to remember: the Conservatives were hired to run this country, not to hide from it.

And these things, they come in threes: out of sight, out of mind could mean out of office.

THE END

With Bob Rae again.
Broadcast Oct. 10, 2006

MERCER: We still have to get that one memorable moment.

RAE: I have an idea.

ABOUT THE AUTHOR

Rick Mercer first came to fame with *Show Me the Button, I'll Push It (Or, Charles Lynch Must Die)*, a one-man show that premiered at the National Arts Centre in 1990 and subsequently toured across Canada. He co-created and was a resident performer on CBC's *This Hour Has 22 Minutes*, created and starred in five seasons of the critically acclaimed *Made in Canada*, and created and starred in the CBC special *Talking to Americans*, which premiered to over 2.7 million viewers on April 1, 2001, making it the most-watched comedy special in Canadian television history. He is now host of *Rick Mercer Report*. Rick is co-chair with Belinda Stronach of the Spread the Net campaign—www.spreadthenet.org—dedicated to preventing the spread of malaria in Africa. His many honours include 21 Geminis and the Governor General's Performing Arts Award. He is from St. John's, Newfoundland and Labrador.